I0285409

Superstition

The Ultimate Guide to Superstitions, Signs, Omens, Symbols, Fortune Telling, Myths, Folklore, and History

© Copyright 2023 - All rights reserved.

The content contained within this book may not be reproduced, duplicated, or transmitted without direct written permission from the author or the publisher.

Under no circumstances will any blame or legal responsibility be held against the publisher, or author, for any damages, reparation, or monetary loss due to the information contained within this book, either directly or indirectly.

Legal Notice:

This book is copyright protected. It is only for personal use. You cannot amend, distribute, sell, use, quote, or paraphrase any part of the content within this book without the consent of the author or publisher.

Disclaimer Notice:

Please note the information contained within this document is for educational and entertainment purposes only. All effort has been executed to present accurate, up-to-date, reliable, and complete information. No warranties of any kind are declared or implied. Readers acknowledge that the author is not engaging in the rendering of legal, financial, medical, or professional advice. The content within this book has been derived from various sources. Please consult a licensed professional before attempting any techniques outlined in this book.

By reading this document, the reader agrees that under no circumstances is the author responsible for any losses, direct or indirect, that are incurred as a result of the use of the information contained within this document, including, but not limited to, errors, omissions, or inaccuracies.

Your Free Gift
(only available for a limited time)

Thanks for getting this book! If you want to learn more about various spirituality topics, then join Mari Silva's community and get a free guided meditation MP3 for awakening your third eye. This guided meditation mp3 is designed to open and strengthen ones third eye so you can experience a higher state of consciousness. Simply visit the link below the image to get started.

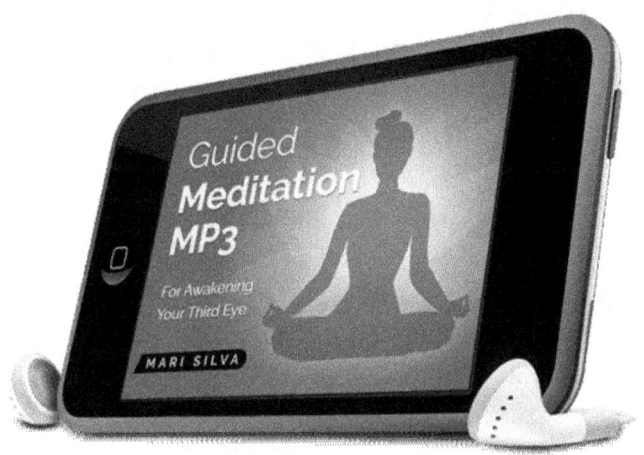

https://spiritualityspot.com/meditation

Table of Contents

INTRODUCTION 1
CHAPTER 1: WHY DO WE BELIEVE IN SUPERSTITIONS? 3
CHAPTER 2: SUPERSTITION AND FORTUNE-TELLING 12
CHAPTER 3: LOOKING FOR SIGNS AND OMENS IN THE SKY 23
CHAPTER 4: THE SYMBOLISM OF COLORS 32
CHAPTER 5: OMENS ABOUT ANIMALS AND PLANTS 42
CHAPTER 6: LUCKY AND UNLUCKY NUMBERS 52
CHAPTER 7: SUPERSTITIONS ABOUT FOOD AND OBJECTS 62
CHAPTER 8: SUPERSTITIONS ABOUT BIRTH AND DEATH 73
CHAPTER 9: WISHES, LUCK, AND FIXING BAD LUCK 83
GLOSSARY OF SUPERSTITIONS, SIGNS, AND OMENS 93
CONCLUSION 100
HERE'S ANOTHER BOOK BY MARI SILVA THAT YOU MIGHT LIKE 102
YOUR FREE GIFT (ONLY AVAILABLE FOR A LIMITED TIME) 103
REFERENCES 104

Introduction

This book will take you on a journey through the fascinating world of superstitions, myths, and omens. For as long as humans have existed, we've looked for meaning in the world around us, and this has led to the creation of a rich and varied tapestry of beliefs and practices. Throughout the ages, we've looked to the sky, the earth, and the animals and plants around us, seeking signs and symbols that might help us make sense of the world. We've turned to fortune-tellers and diviners to try and see into the future, and we've used objects, food, and even numbers to bring luck and ward off misfortune. From the ancient belief in omens to the modern-day practice of Feng Shui, we've turned to these beliefs to help us navigate the ups and downs of life.

But why do we believe in these things? What about the human psyche makes us so susceptible to superstition? This book will answer this question by exploring the psychological and cultural factors that contribute to our belief in superstitions and examining the role fear, uncertainty, and the need for control have shaped our beliefs. You'll understand how people's upbringing, environment, and life experiences shape their beliefs and practices.

You will also get to take a closer look at the role of nature and the environment in our superstitions. The shapes of clouds, the patterns of bird flights, and the colors of the sky all hold meaning and significance in cultures around the world. Similarly, the behavior of animals and the properties of plants have been used to predict the future, offer protection, and even help with healing. You can also study the many different ways that superstitions have been used throughout history, from the ancient civilizations of Egypt and Greece to the modern-day world of horoscopes and lucky charms. Keep reading to explore the fascinating symbolism of colors, animals, and numbers, and delve into the many different superstitions around objects, food, and even birth and death.

Overall, this book offers a comprehensive look at the world of superstitions, myths, and omens; by its end, you'll have a deeper understanding of this rich and complex world. Whether you're a skeptic or a true believer, you will find something intriguing and thought-provoking in these pages. So, if you're ready to explore this mystical world and unlock the secrets of our collective beliefs, this book is the perfect place to start.

Chapter 1: Why Do We Believe in Superstitions?

With the technological advancements and scientific discoveries of today's day and age, it is hard to believe that many people still strongly believe in seemingly irrational superstitions. However, you might be surprised to learn about the self-fulfilling nature of these beliefs and the psychology behind them. Nearly all superstitions practiced in different parts of the world today stem from interesting pieces of lore, stories, and myths. Some of them even seemed perfectly rational and useful at the time of their creation.

This chapter will set out to demystify what superstitions are and that they are *not just* sayings that your granny dropped into any conversation as a cautionary tale. We'll delve deep into why many superstitions appear true – even though they aren't backed by scientific evidence. You'll understand why many people believe in them and how individuals who don't believe in omens and good luck charms can become superstitious too!

This chapter also explores some of the most internationally widespread superstitions, explains where and how they originated, and highlights the differences and similarities of superstitions across cultures. You will learn how anthropologists define superstitions, why they study them, and how they classify them. Finally, you'll understand the interconnected nature of superstitions, myths, and folklore and how they can give us insight into how people used to think, act, and interact with the world around them.

What Are Superstitions?

Have you ever walked into an elevator and found that the building has a 12B, 14A, or M floor rather than a 13th? Was the last plane you took missing a 13th or 17th row?

Were you ever told that you shouldn't have an early birthday celebration? How would people react if you opened an umbrella indoors? Do you hear the words "break your mother's back" ringing in your ears every time you accidentally step on a crack?

The number 13 is considered unlucky in most parts of the world, while the number 17 carries the title of "bad luck" in Brazil, Italy, and a few other countries. It is also generally believed that early birthday wishes and celebrations and the act of opening an umbrella indoors will attract bad luck.

These are all superstitions you've heard all your life, regardless of how superstitious you or your family are. They are commonly held beliefs that everyone follows despite not knowing the real reason behind them.

There isn't a single definition that can be attributed to the word superstition. It is a way of thinking and refers to how people perceive certain events and happenings. Superstitious people generally believe in fate, luck, and other supernatural forces and associate them with particular symbols or happenings. Superstitious individuals generally feel the need to reduce feelings of uncertainty by finding ways to predict the unknown. This means that an individual's personal beliefs and experiences shape their superstitions, which they would then accidentally or intentionally pass on to their children.

For instance, if you notice that you seem to have the best day at work whenever you see a butterfly on your way there, your brain's reward system will get activated each time you come across a butterfly. You'll automatically expect your day to go smoothly, and so will subconsciously do everything in your power to make it happen.

On the other hand, if you believe in the black cat superstition and come across one in the morning, you'll automatically assume that your day is ruined. Even if you don't necessarily self-sabotage, you won't do anything to give yourself a good day, either. If you run into problems or conflicts -expected in any work environment - you won't do anything to fix them because "it would be of no use." If you face problems when you're expecting things to work out for the best, this will encourage you to take positive remedial actions. Superstitions are self-fulfilling because people's beliefs influence their attitudes and behaviors, which shape their actions.

You might also start believing in a superstition just because someone pointed it out. Say you're heading out to work, and your neighbor warns you about the crow sitting at your windowsill all morning. He claims that crows are bad luck and that you must watch out. You brush it off, but it still lingers in your mind. There's traffic on your way to work, and you arrive late to an important meeting. You tell yourself this can happen to anyone and put it behind you. Then, you get into an argument with your co-worker, and to top it all off, you take the wrong exit on your way home - and now you have to spend an extra 30 minutes on the road! Normally, you'd tell yourself that everyone has bad days. However, now that you know that the crow you saw in the morning attracts bad luck, you might start to believe that the superstition is true.

Why Do People Believe in Superstitions?

Each culture, or even family, has its own superstitions ingrained into the minds, behaviors, and daily interactions of its people. Some superstitions are even popular on a global level. If there is no scientific backing to these beliefs and associations, why do so many people believe in them?

Superstitious beliefs and behaviors can generally imbue a sense of direction and control in those who engage in them. The thought that the future, whether long- or short-term, is highly unpredictable makes many people feel anxious. To them, using external factors and occurrences to gain insight into the future or influence certain results helps them feel at ease. This explains why most superstitions originated during periods of wars, calamities, and economic crises, which cause feelings of uncertainty to arise among people.

According to The Conversation academic article, superstitious individuals are more likely to develop positive mental attitudes. They're also prone to making irrational decisions led by notions like fate and good or bad luck.

Superstitious people don't only look for signs in the outside world, but they also believe that they can do certain things to attract good fortune. For instance, they might carry charms, wear certain jewelry or clothes, or prefer specific numbers or colors on important days or when making significant decisions. They might also avoid doing specific things or wearing certain items altogether because they associate them with bad luck.

Superstitions in the World of Sports

Superstitions are very popular in sports, especially when things get competitive. You might be surprised that around 80% of athletes follow superstitious regimens before competing. Most athletes find that these behaviors help reduce their anxiety and stress and give them a better sense of control over the outcome and factors beyond their control.

Even though each player and game has their own particular superstitions, there are commonalities. For instance, equestrians and gymnasts think they'll feel and appear more prepared when they look well-dressed and put together. Footballers and other athletes might pray for good outcomes. Many athletes also engage in personal superstitions, such as wearing lucky clothes or carrying charms around. Some players also dedicate certain sporting gear to competitions.

If you're into basketball, you might already be aware of Michael Jordan's superstitious behaviors. He wears lucky shorts under his team's kit. Björn Borg, the world-renowned tennis player, was known to wear the same branded shirts. Rafael Nadal also follows a pre-game ritual that helps boost his performance.

While these rituals won't directly steer the outcomes in the athletes' favor, they can actually help them perform better. Since said rituals and practices can help ease anxiety and make athletes feel more empowered, they'd be able to focus better on their performance than their thoughts and feelings. Stress and anxiety are known to hinder people's performance. If an athlete fails to engage in their superstitious behaviors before they perform, they'll feel anxious and worried, which then becomes evident on the scoreboard.

Internationally Widespread Superstitions

Even though the general idea and structure of certain superstitions are shared by many countries worldwide, the meaning behind them and the consequences that follow if engaged with them might vary.

The following are some internationally widespread superstitions, their origins, and their similarities and differences across cultures:

Touch/Knock on Wood

In many cultures worldwide, people believe that touching or knocking on a piece of wood can help free them of bad luck or attract good fortune. The phrase touch or knock on wood originated in 19th-century Britain, with little information on the story behind it. However, most explanations point back to the Celts, who thought trees served as homes for deities and other celestial creatures. The Celts thought that knocking on trees was a way to show gratitude to the spirits in exchange for abundance or to call on them for guidance and protection. Some people believe this practice also helped them get rid of bad luck and keep evil spirits from finding out about people's abundance so they wouldn't reverse their good fortune. The act of touching or knocking on wood can also be traced back to Christianity, as many historians suggest that wood is associated with the cross of Christ's crucifixion.

Many others suggest this superstition doesn't go that far back in history. According to Steve Roud, a British folklorist, the act of touching wood came from a 19th-century game of tag. In Tiggy Touchwood, children who touched any piece of wood during the game couldn't be caught by the other players. With the growing popularity of the game among both children and adults, wood became known as a source of protection, and therefore, the phrase "touch wood" was incorporated into the British vernacular.

While no one knows where the superstition came from, it is still among the most popular shared beliefs worldwide. Many cultures even have their own spin on the practice. For instance, in addition to knocking on wood twice, Turkish people tug at their ears to fight off jinxes, and in Italy, people say "touch iron" rather than wood when they're tempted to partake in risky behaviors.

Toasting with Water

According to the Mess Night Manual of naval history, people who toast using a glass of water will die by drowning. Along with water, soft drinks and liqueurs can bring bad luck. This superstition can also be traced back to Greek mythology, as ancient Greeks avoided toasting with water out of respect to the River Lethe. Legend says that those who die sail to the Underworld via this river, so toasting with water would imply that you wish death by drowning on yourself or those you are toasting.

Ancient Greeks also thought that using a glass vessel of water while toasting was an invitation to the deities to cast a series of bad luck upon you. The act of clicking a glass of water is practiced by many cultures to this day.

Black Cats and Birds

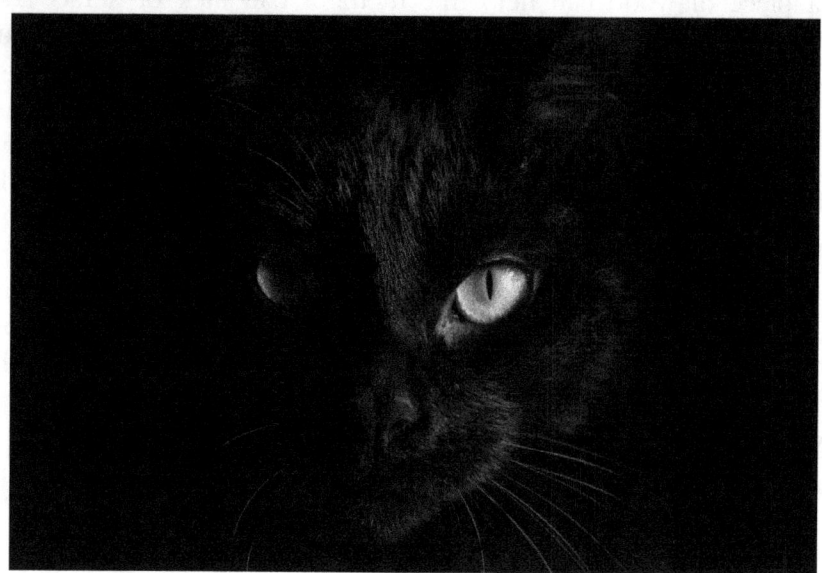

Black cat.
https://unsplash.com/photos/0FQneB1VjaM?utm_source=unsplash&utm_medium=referral&utm_content=creditShareLink

Unfortunately, many widespread superstitions impact the lives of other innocent creatures. Black cats, for instance, were found to have lower adoption rates than cats of other colors. They're also often treated differently, discriminated against, overlooked, and even abused due to superstitions that they are carriers of bad luck. These beliefs are most pronounced around Halloween, as the poor furry animals are associated with witches. Many people around the world believe that their day will take a turn for the worse if they come across a black cat.

Black cats, however, are not the only creatures linked to bad omens. For example, South Koreans strongly believe that spotting a black crow would immediately result in bad fortune, and they also think they're messengers of death. In the UK, ravens are believed to predict impending doom. There's another superstition that the British monarchy will fall if the number of ravens spotted on the Tower of London, at any given moment, is less than 6. Scottish and Irish people think that ill fortune will come their way if they see a single magpie;

however, they believe they're good to go if they come across two or more of this type of bird.

How Anthropologists Classify Superstitions

Anthropologists study superstitions and the history behind them to gain insight into the differences between cultures, understand how people think, and learn more about the different ways individuals try to make sense of the world around them. Anthropologists are interested in discovering how and why these beliefs and perceptions are passed down from one generation to another.

They define superstitions as beliefs and practices not supported by logical or rational reasoning or scientific evidence and are purely shaped by group or individualistic beliefs, experiences, or traditions. They also generally classify superstitions into three categories: interpreting signs, magic superstitions, and conversion superstitions. How superstitions are classified depends on the relevant practices, behaviors, beliefs, and eminence in a cultural context. In most cases, superstitions are classified as aspects of larger spiritual or religious systems. However, some people think they aren't elements of organized belief systems.

Interpreting signs and superstitions refer to superstitious beliefs and practices that are content-based. These superstitions require interpreting and analyzing events, occurrences, symbols, or signs as omens of bad or good fortune. An example of this type of superstition would be carrying a horseshoe around to attract good fortune.

Magic superstitions are associated with practices and rituals used to attract good fortune and steer bad luck away. An example of this type of superstition would be carrying a charm to protect yourself from evil forces and harm or performing a certain ritual before tests or competitions to steer the results in your favor.

Conversion superstitions refer to the idea that a certain happening or practice can undo bad luck or convert it into good fortune. For instance, a superstitious person who steps on a crack in the sidewalk would take it as a sign of imminent bad luck. However, they might throw salt over their shoulder to attract good luck and cancel out the previous omen.

Anthropologists are careful to account for the social and cultural contexts in which the superstitions occur because even if the practices are the same across different cultures, their meanings may differ. They also observe the roles they play in the lives of people and the amount of influence that these superstitions have over their actions.

How Superstitions, Myths, and Folklore Are Interconnected

The terms superstitions, myths, and folklore are often used interchangeably, which is why many think they all refer to old, whimsical tales. These terms indeed feature imaginative characters and storylines; however, they all aim to fulfill a significant purpose: to explain the world and answer the fundamental questions of life.

Back then, people didn't have the knowledge and technology to make sense of the world around them. They didn't understand why basic phenomena occurred, so they had to find other ways to explain them. They didn't realize that droughts were caused by environmental changes, for instance, and therefore assumed that they'd upset the god of rainfall. They didn't know the reasons behind their ailments, so blaming it on the black crow they'd seen earlier seemed reasonable at the time.

Each of these terms has unique characteristics; however, they're all similar in how their significance hasn't withered with time. They're also connected in how they transmit cultural traditions, values, ideologies, practices, and beliefs across generations. They each preserve cultural elements differently, giving insight into how people used to think and act and reflecting how individuals used to approach and interact with the world around them. You can tell a lot about a culture by reading into its myths and folklore and exploring its superstitions.

How Are They Different?

Myths are traditional tales that provide answers to basic questions that people have about life, creation, and the world. They were commonly shared orally in efforts to explain supernatural happenings, certain phenomena, and mysteries. They were also used to back up cultural traditions and reinforce norms and values among people. Myths that revolved around deities and other spiritual creatures were sacred and still influence several aspects of many cultures to this day. They often explained certain events in light of spiritual beliefs, such as the occurrence of misfortunes due to upset gods or conflicts between them.

Myths and the personages featured in the myth influence many superstitions, such as toasting with water. Superstitions are merely elements of myths and are influenced by them – the terms are not interchangeable. While the former are traditional stories that comprise characters and events, superstitions are beliefs that *might or might not* have been featured in myths.

While myths often revolved around deities and explained how cultures and peoples originated, folklore revolved around people and other living creatures. Mythologies explored life through a spiritual lens, and folktales captured the essence and commonalities of daily life. Folklore gives us information about how people used to live. These tales explore common challenges and conflicts that people faced at the time and what they did to cope. Superstitions are popular elements in cultural stories and folktales.

Now that you have read this chapter, you understand why many people, regardless of how well-educated and intelligent they are, still believe in superstitions and allow them to influence various aspects of their lives. Superstitious practices give people a greater sense of control over their lives and help alleviate their anxiety toward unpredictable situations. Superstitions generally offer a sense of comfort and security. Many cultures also use these beliefs as ways to introduce and develop cultural values and norms. Superstitions are double-edged swords. They are mind tricks that can either encourage us to work hard or succumb to the status quo. Hard work brings good fortune, so don't fret the next time you are seated in the 13th row or step on a crack in the sidewalk.

Chapter 2: Superstition and Fortune-Telling

Fortune telling refers to the craft used to interpret the future or identify the influences of past and present actions. It's also part of a larger group of practices called divination. The latter is used to unveil hidden knowledge through magic and intuitive awareness. While the concepts of divination and fortune-telling are often used interchangeably, divination often reveals information on a much larger scale. Nevertheless, both fortune-telling and divination are often linked to superstition. This chapter explores the connection between divination and superstition. It also provides popular and simple divination methods suggested for beginners, including tea-leaf reading, scrying, tarot reading, and automatic writing.

The Connection between Superstition and Fortune Telling

Fortune-telling involves looking for meaning in patterns and symbols. Many of these patterns came from observing nature and the causes of the events in nature. Even in ancient times, people were closely affiliated with nature and what it was doing and trying to make sense of it. While (to the untrained eye) it might seem impossible to make sense of random patterns, the unconscious mind is very good at finding meaning even when there seemingly isn't any. A great example is people's ability to see faces and other images in living beings and non-living objects around them. This phenomenon is responsible for the birth of many superstitions too. When seeing something they couldn't interpret, people found alternate interpretations for shapes and symbols and linked them to known objects with similar characteristics. Throughout history, the working and lower classes often could not conceive the reasoning behind misfortunes and other sudden events. Since these seemingly inexplicable events made them feel that they don't have control over their lives, they simply found a different explanation for them, thereby taking back the desired control. Whatever signs or symbols they noticed just before the events were linked to the newfound explanations. If their subconscious associates an object or animal with a particular event, they interpret seeing the latter as a sign of that event, which is also just how fortune telling or divination in general works.

Symbols and Fortune Telling

Whichever divination method you use, being a fortune teller enables you to become a medium through which you gather information. You can garner knowledge about yourself or someone else seeking information about their future, present or past. For beginners, start practicing by divining for yourself first before you undertake to guide others. This will give you the experience of building a connection between your tools, that is, the method of choice and your intuition. Whether seeking information about love, finances, or spirituality, you'll need to learn how to fine-tune your readings.

In this chapter, you'll be given several techniques, each requiring you to decipher messages by looking for shapes and symbols. Whatever you see will create a symbolism in your mind, which will help form a connection between the explanation in your unconscious mind and the image in your conscious mind. This connection is the key to deciphering divinatory messages. In the subsequent chapter, you'll read about the symbolism of different superstitions. Interpreting these symbols is just like fortune telling. Once again, your mind interprets a sign it sees and links it to a belief hidden in your subconscious.

Popular Divination Methods

Fortune telling is an ancient art. Countless archeological records of different divination methods were used in Ancient Egypt, Babylonia, and China as early as 4000 BC. Roman writers have also recorded the divinatory practices of the ancient Druids. While most divinatory practices were suppressed for centuries, they resurfaced in the 19th and 20th centuries and gained popularity again. Fortune-telling methods have come a long way, from entertaining parlor games to tools for gaining self-awareness and spiritual enlightenment. Below are several popular and simple divination methods you can try to learn more about your future, fortune, and superstitious associations.

Scrying

Scrying is a technique that involves looking into a reflective surface and using it as a tool for gaining insight into different situations or finding lost items. Traditionally, scrying was done through a crystal ball or the moon. However, the practice has since evolved, and nowadays, you can use smoke, candle flame, a wood-burning fire, a large body of calm water (like a pond or lake), scrying bowls, small bowls with water, coffee grounds, and tea leaves. Not only that, but you can also use different pieces of nature or your environment to discern spiritual messages. Any object or living creature you see around you can be used as a scrying tool. In fact, most superstitions have originated from people's ideas when looking at a particular object or animal while scrying unconsciously. Besides answering simple questions, scrying can also help you find answers to tough questions and resolve challenging issues. You can find clarity in your relationships or learn about the consequences of your current actions. Or, you can scry to relax your mind and dissipate everyday worries. You only need your preferred scrying tool and relaxation techniques. Once you have those, you can start scrying.

Instructions:
1. Start by finding a quiet place where you won't be disturbed. Light a candle and turn off all the artificial lights and devices that might distract you. If you prefer, burn incense, put on some relaxing music, or use anything else you find helpful for relaxing. Your body should be upright, your shoulders relaxed but not slouching. Close your eyes and bring your focus to your breathing.
2. Set your scrying tool in front of you. Calm your mind and body until you reach a light trance-like state. Your mind should be focused solely on your intent. Some of the best ways to get into

this state are mindfulness or breathing techniques, mantra repetition, and yoga.
3. When you've found the stillness within, you should now feel your senses radiating with spiritual energy and focus on your scrying tool.
4. Direct your gaze softly on your tool and keep an open mind to whatever thoughts or images the scrying tool inspires. You might not receive an answer to the question you've asked. If this happens, you were looking for something else deep in your subconscious, except you weren't consciously aware of it. Other times, the answer you get will be indirectly related to your question - you will just have to figure out how.

The key to mastering scrying is trusting your intuition. While this might sound pretty simple, it often requires a lot of practice, especially if you don't have experience using your intuition and divination tools. When you scry, you are communicating with your subconscious mind, asking for information stored there. This is beyond the reach of your conscious and your ordinary sense, so you aren't aware of them. Your subconscious will, however, project the messages onto the tool. They'll appear as images and thoughts you recognize, making your conscious mind aware of them. You'll need as much concentration as you can muster to do this. If you have trouble focusing, try practicing it late in the evening. At this time, you're less likely to be disturbed, and your mind will likely be less likely to get stuck on unrelated ideas.

You can still practice during the day if you don't have time or feel too tired to scry late at night. In fact, you can scry wherever you are doing something that requires you to stay still or focus on a specific task. For example, when you shower, you focus on taking a shower, and you're already shutting everything else out. Without realizing it, you're entering the trance-like state required for scrying. Because of this, moments like these are perfect for practicing scrying. Just look at the surfaces around you, and your intuition will come up with something.

Tea-Leaf Reading

Tea leaf reading depicting a flying bird and a dog.
MochaSwirl, Public domain, via Wikimedia Commons:
<https://commons.wikimedia.org/wiki/File:Tea_leaf_reading.jpg>

Tea-leaf reading, or tasseomancy, is a specific form of scrying. It is a relatively new method and has gained popularity in the past century. Like any other scrying technique, reading tea leaves requires you to use a surface to translate messages from your subconscious. You'll need teacups, a saucer or plate, and tea for tea leaf reading. When choosing your teacup, choose a rounded one with a shallow bowl and a large handle. It should be white or pale in color to create a bigger contrast between its surface and the tea leaves. This will make it easier to see the shapes and symbols and interpret their messages. When it comes to the brew, you'll need loose-leaf tea, and you can use herbal blends and blends with spices. The texture of the leaves should be medium, not too fine, but not too coarse either.

Instructions:

1. Place a teaspoon of loose leaves into the cup and pour boiling water over them. Steep for 3-4 minutes. Alternatively, you can brew the tea in a teapot without a built-in strainer. The leaves will need to go into the cup along with the water. If you opt for this

method, stir the tea before pouring, so the leaves will be equally distributed in the brew.

2. After pouring the brew (or steeping the leaves in the cup), let the leaves settle a little more. When the tea has cooled to the temperature you like, take the cup with your non-dominant hand (use your left hand if you're right-handed and your right if you're left-handed).

3. Sip your tea slowly. Take your time enjoying it. This is crucial for relaxing before divination. Drink your tea in a calm environment. Turn off any device that might distract you, and take a few minutes to clear your mind.

4. As you sip your tea, start focusing on your intent. Do you have a specific question you want to be answered? If not, try to formulate one. Try aiming for a question that looks at the broader picture. For example, instead of asking: "What should I do tomorrow morning?" Try asking questions like: "Should I look for a job tomorrow morning?"

5. If you don't have a question, don't worry. For beginners, it's also acceptable to read tea leaves without questions. You'll get a general reading of your future, which is also great for practicing this divination method.

6. When only a tiny amount of liquid is left in the cup, swirl it in an anticlockwise direction. Repeat this motion two more times to spread the leaves around the sides of the cup.

7. Place a paper towel on the saucer and slowly turn the cup upside down, setting it on the saucer. Let the excess liquid drain out, tap the bottom of the cup three times, and turn it over.

8. Hold the cup by its side. Its handle should point towards your heart. Look at the contents of the cup from several angles. Study any symbols or particular shapes that catch your attention. Besides the images formed by the leaves, you should also look at the forms created by the white surfaces of the cup.

9. Take your time looking at how the shapes are formed. They might not look like anything, but don't discard any thoughts or images they remind you of. The images may not make sense to your conscious mind, but your intuition will find the hidden meanings. If you listen to it, it will translate these messages into your consciousness.

While there are no rules to tea leaf reading, there are a few things to remember. For example, the placement of the shapes can indicate specific areas of life. Shapes closer to cup handles are typically associated with family, home, and one's self-image. These areas might show you issues with which you are currently struggling. You should read the leaves in a clockwise direction, starting from the rim on the left of the handle. Going in a downward spiral, slowly turn the cup and continue observing the leaves until you reach the bottom.

Shapes near the cup's rim are linked to the immediate future. Whatever you see in them will be related to the next few days. Images in the middle of the cup correlate to events and situations that'll occur within a couple of weeks. The shapes at the bottom are associated with events due within the next month.

While there are symbol charts for tea leaves, the most effective way to get results is to listen to your intuitive meanings of the images. For example, if you can see a book in the images, this could be a message related to a new chapter in your life. Or, it could be associated with your love of reading, depending on what your gut tells you. While letters in the tea leaves are traditionally linked to important people in one's life, they could also relate to a place you want or will visit in the future. You should also pay attention to how the symbols are linked to each other. Some symbols have different meanings when they appear alongside others.

Firstly, you should only focus on deciphering messages from individual symbols. When you've mastered this, you can try to create a story from the different associations you discover in the tea leaves. According to lore, tea leaves can only uncover positive outcomes. Consequently, you should only focus on positive events and situations and avoid asking questions about the negative ones.

Tarot Reading

Tarot card reading.
https://unsplash.com/photos/D3SzBCAeMhQ?utm_source=unsplash&utm_medium=referral&utm_content=creditShareLink

Tarot reading is a well-known divination method using Tarot cards with predetermined meanings and connecting them to one's subconscious. Each card has its own story, which is part of a much larger picture. To master tarot reading for divination, you'll need to learn about the primary meanings of the cards. Tarot decks consist of 78 cards, divided into the Major Arcana and the Minor Arcana. The 22 cards of the Major Arcana tell the story of a journey (commonly known as the Fool's journey). The 56 cards of the Minor Arcana display nuanced details of one's journey, situation, or outcomes. Tarot cards won't reveal exact scenarios from the future. However, they offer guidance for interpreting future events based on your thoughts, actions, and outside influences. Besides tapping into the general meaning of each card, Tarot reading also relies on your intuition. When looking at the cards you pull, you interpret them based on what your subconscious tells you about them. This encourages you to practice self-awareness and learn more about your deepest thoughts, desires, and needs.

Instructions:

1. Prepare your body and mind by relaxing. After clearing your mind, start focusing on a question. Avoid asking questions that require passive answers. For example, instead of beginning your question with "Should I...," start with "What do I need to learn about..."

2. Try to ask a question that shows the broader picture, so the cards can illuminate a journey you need to take to reach the foreseen outcome. You can ask the cards why you're feeling anxious about superstitions. Or you can ask for guidance to understand your beliefs and inquire about what areas of life you should focus on to move past obstacles and superstitions.
3. Once you've thought of your questions (beginners should start practicing with just one), place the Tarot deck into your hands and shuffle it. You can use the overhead shuffle method and hold the deck in one hand and use the other to take cards from one place in the deck to another one. You can also cut the deck by dividing it into smaller piles, mixing the order of the piles, and combining them into one. Another way to shuffle is through the sweeping method. This involves laying out all the cards on the table, gathering them into a pile, and arranging them into a neat deck.
4. Pull a card from the deck. The easiest way to do this is to divide the deck on your left and draw the card from the top. You can also fan them out and pick the one you feel drawn to. The latter is particularly effective for connecting to your intuition.
5. As a beginner, start practicing with one card. Once you've learned how to interpret the messages of one card reading, you can venture into pulling several cards and doing popular spreads.
6. Once you've pulled a card, lay it face down. Take a deep breath and turn it over. Look at its imagery and words, and think about what they mean to you. Don't overthink it. Whatever thought comes to mind first comes from your conscious, and this is what you're looking for when using your intuition for Tarot readings.
7. If you can't find any meaning to the card you've pulled, refer to their predetermined symbolism. These can be great stepping stones for learning to decipher what the cards are trying to tell you.

One-card pulls are the easiest ways to get into Tarot readings. You can pull a card daily to strengthen your intuitive connection to the cards. They can answer simple questions, and if you're interested in getting more details, you can pull three cards. And when you're ready to do spreads, you can do a five-card layout for intuition and clarity or a seven-card reading for a more in-depth analysis of the different influences on your future outcomes.

Automatic Writing

Automatic writing is another popular way of fortune-telling. Like Tarot cards, writing can also become a tool for extracting knowledge from your subconscious. Or you can use it to exchange messages with the spiritual world. You will only need a pen and paper and channel your intention to let messages flow through you without you consciously dictating this process. Alternatively, you can use modern writing methods (mobile devices, computer keyboards, etc.). Still, the traditional way is more likely to help you connect with your subconscious, and the more successful you will be in deciphering the future through automatic writing.

Instructions:

1. Start by finding a quiet spot without distractions. Get a piece of paper and a pen or pencil, and remove any clutter from the space in front of you. Prepare yourself by meditating or doing any other mindfulness technique. The goal is to relax and start focusing on your intention.

2. When you've cleared your mind, think about the question you want to ask about the future. Try to formulate the inquiries as simply as you can. For starters, only focus on the most pressing question. You can address the question to yourself or a spiritual guide you want to contact.

3. Relax some more by taking a couple of deep breaths. When you're ready, put the pen into your hand. Let it touch the paper without consciously directing its movement. If you feel the need to control your writing, put the pen down and clear your mind before continuing.

4. Try not to consciously write but let your hand do whatever feels natural. Let it write automatically without looking at the paper. Close your eyes if it helps you avoid looking at whatever your hand is writing. Take your time. It might take a few minutes for the thoughts to start flowing from your subconscious.

5. When you've finished your session, look at the paper. At first, what you've written might not make sense, or your writing might look like you've scribbled random words, numbers, or pictures).

However, you should still try to interpret it. Consider what each word or symbol means to you and what they might mean concerning your question.

6. If you haven't been able to decipher enough to answer your inquiry, don't worry. It sometimes takes a couple of attempts for beginners to get an answer to a question. Finding relaxation techniques that suit your personality often helps speed up the process. And when you start receiving messages, remember to be open-minded about them.

Chapter 3: Looking for Signs and Omens in the Sky

In days of old, people believed the elements of the sky held indications and portents concerning their destiny. From the stars to birds' flights and clouds, within their imagination, there has always been a curiosity and excitement associated with divining one's fate via signs and omens in the sky. Ancient cultures embraced nature and looked to it for guidance and knowledge of things beyond human insight. As time has passed and we have developed an understanding of our physical world, these ancient beliefs have become something of a novelty or curiosity. Yet through all shifting perspectives of society, there continues to be fascination within every culture as to what is hidden in the blue expanse which towers above us each morning.

What Are Omens?

Omens are signs or signals from the natural world that are believed by some to be indicators of future events. They can take a variety of forms, such as sounds, objects, or other physical things. Many cultures consider it to be a way of understanding the divine will of the gods and other supernatural forces. In some societies, omens are seen as good luck symbols; in others, they are more associated with fear and superstition.

Omens have been studied and documented extensively throughout human history. Ancient Chinese texts describe how omens were used to predict important events such as battles, floods, and weather patterns.

The ancient Greeks also had a system for interpreting natural occurrences and seeing prophetic messages from the gods. In cultures around the world, birds have been associated with omens. In particular, seeing a white bird is said to bring good luck, while sighting a black bird is often seen as bad news.

In writing and literature, omens have long been incorporated into stories to create suspense or foreshadow upcoming events. Some examples include Shakespeare's Macbeth or Homer's Odyssey, where supernatural interventions act as warnings or portents of what is to come. Even today, some still believe that certain objects or occurrences can carry special meaning about their personal fate or fortune and use these as guidance for their decisions in life.

Overall, an omen is an occurrence or sign someone interprets as having a deeper spiritual meaning than how it may appear on the surface. According to different beliefs and traditions, it may bring either positive or negative outcomes depending on its form and context. Regardless of how it is interpreted, it reminds us that unseen powers beyond our control shape our lives.

Good Omen vs. Bad Omens

Part of human culture for thousands of years, omens are believed to be signs from a higher power that foretell the future and can influence people's decisions and behavior. The idea behind omens is that they can provide insight into what is to come, and some people take them very seriously. There is a distinction between good and bad omens in many cultures, with the former being seen as favorable indicators and the latter as unfavorable.

Good omens often involve natural or supernatural events seen as positive or hopeful for the future. A rainbow could be seen as a sign of good luck or protection from danger, while sightings of certain animals, such as eagles, were considered auspicious events that would bring about success or fortune. Other examples include dragonflies, which signify change or transformation; ladybugs, which symbolize new beginnings; and four-leaf clovers, which are thought to bring good luck. These symbols all offer hope and promise a desirable outcome in whatever situation they appear in.

On the other hand, bad omens indicate undesirable outcomes and typically involve darker elements like death or misfortune. In some cultures, the appearance of certain animals, such as bats, was considered an omen of bad luck or death. The same was true of black cats crossing one's path. Other symbols, like a broken mirror, were also believed to bring about seven years' worth of bad luck, while sneezing three times was viewed as a warning of imminent danger ahead.

What Could Have Influenced People's Beliefs?

Many believe these associations stem from ancient spiritual traditions that sought to make sense of the unknown by connecting them with known phenomena in nature. The fact that certain animals were rarer than others likely made them more mysterious and thus associated with greater power or significance in some cases. Likewise, colors such as those seen in rainbows had strong symbolic meanings since they could not be explained by natural means alone. People also attributed meaning to physical phenomena such as storms because they seemed so powerful and out of their control – something they attributed to divine intervention rather than just mere happenstance. Additionally, superstitions passed down through generations may have further solidified these beliefs. Regardless, it appears that humans will continue finding ways to interpret their environment and seek out meanings beyond what is tangible in this world.

Mindfulness Exercise

Learning to understand the omens present in everyday life can be a helpful tool for staying focused on the present moment and noticing any signs or blessings in our lives. To begin, set aside some time each day to focus on small moments. This could be five minutes of positive affirmations, deep breathing exercises, or mindful meditation. This will help to clear your mind and leave you more open to receiving any messages conveyed through symbols and signs. As you go about your day, pay attention to coincidences, flashes of inspiration, and impressions that float into your mind. These insights could be hints about how to move forward with a complicated situation or offer insight into future possibilities. You should also learn to listen to both with your ears and heart. Consider all forms of communication as possible omens. Whether it is a meaningful conversation at the park or words on a billboard as you're driving by, it can help inform decisions and situations in life. Finally, make a note of how these signs are helping you notice subtle shifts within yourself to take action through any potential opportunities presented to you.

Mindfulness exercise to get and understand omens:

1. **Find a quiet space:** Start by finding a quiet place where you can be alone and undisturbed. It could be your bedroom, balcony, or even a park if you have access to one. Spend some undistracted time in this space and just focus on yourself being present.
2. **Take slow deep breaths:** Once you are in the right environment, take some slow deep breaths through your nose with your eyes closed. This will help clear away all the thoughts that may come up from the busyness of life or anxiety about what happens later on today or tomorrow. Focus only on breathing for at least five minutes, allowing yourself to relax and become more aware of the present moment.
3. **Become aware of your body:** After taking those deep breaths, start to become aware of your body and the sensations it is experiencing. Notice how your feet feel against the ground or if there is a breeze brushing against your skin. Pay attention to every detail you can sense at that moment without judgment or expectations. This will help bring you back into the present and allow you to be more attuned to potential omens around you.
4. **Open up to what's around you:** Now that you are connected with your own body, open up to what's around you. Take some time to observe everything that is happening in that environment, from people's conversations to birds flying nearby. Let your gaze linger on each thing without trying to analyze or understand it. Just observe from a distance and see what feelings you get from these things around you.
5. **Notice any meaningful signs:** After a few minutes of observing, start to pay attention to any meaningful signs that may appear. These could be anything from a bird chirping at an unexpected time to a sudden wind blowing through the trees. Tune into these moments and take mental notes of them to remember them later if necessary.
6. **Reflect on the possible interpretations**: After taking note of all the potential omens, sit back and reflect on what they could mean. Remember that omens are open to interpretation and have different meanings for different people. Don't be hard on

yourself if you don't get clear answers immediately. Just take some time to ponder the possible interpretations of these signs, and make sure you keep an open mind when doing so.

7. **Take action:** Once you have reflected on all the omens and their meanings, it's time to decide what you should do with this information. Depending on what type of omen it is, there may be an action or decision that needs to be taken for your life to move forward positively. Don't be afraid to take risks and trust your gut when it comes to making decisions, as these omens can often be a sign of something great that's about to come into your life.

By following this mindfulness exercise, you should be able to become more aware of the present and pick up any potential omens. Remember to keep an open mind when interpreting them, take action if necessary and stay focused on the here and now so that you don't miss out on any important signs or messages.

Celestial Omens

1. Spotting a Shooting Star

Seeing a shooting star is thought to be an omen of good luck by cultures the world over. This superstition likely originated in the celebrations that used to occur when a bright "shooting star" was seen. Ancient Roman and Greek folklore linked stars with fate and fortune, so sighting one was often regarded as a sign that good luck was soon to come. In some cultures, it even symbolizes wishes being granted. Across cultures, seeing a shooting star is still widely viewed as a good omen and calls for hope, faith, and perseverance on our paths in life. No matter your background or beliefs, we can all bask in the beauty of watching a shooting star light up across the night sky and remember to keep our sense of wonderment alive.

2. Halo around the Moon

Seeing a halo around the moon has been an omen of bad weather for centuries, with tales about its meaning varying from culture to culture. The origins of this concept can be traced back to ancient Greece, where it was believed that Zeus, the chief god, would shoot arrows at the sky to produce rain or hail. Many cultures adopted this belief from there, seeing a lunar halo as a sign of Zeus' anger. Different cultures interpret its meaning differently; some say it foretells storms, while others believe it will bring luck and good fortune. However, what is widely accepted is that when a halo appears around the moon, there will be some kind of weather event coming in. Though science hasn't yet proved exactly what causes such halos to appear around the moon, one thing is certain: if you see one, you better get ready for something wild!

3. Spotting All Five Visible Planets

The inexplicable sight of all five visible planets in the sky at once is considered an omen across many cultures that spans generations and galaxies. An ethereal beauty, this rare occurrence is an indication of fortuitous events. The origins of this belief stem from ancient texts and cultures that incorporated astrology into their ways of living and mythologies from tales of folklore and civilizations from long ago, and people began to recognize how powerful figures in the sky could be to our lives. Believing in the cosmic power held within each planet's unique energy, stargazers have been drawn to the magnificent sign all five visible planets represent when they appear in a unified display. Aptly dubbed the Grand Conjunction, a special moment like this gives hope, signs of blessing, and faith that brighter times are ahead.

4. Seeing Sun and Moon Together

Seeing the sun and moon together in the sky has long been seen as a symbol of good fortune and wealth across many cultures and societies. Dating back to ancient times, such an occurrence was believed to have divine origins, with some believing it was an omen sent from the gods themselves. Some cultures viewed it as a sign that they would be blessed with abundant wealth, while others saw it as a warning against pride or overreach. In Chinese astrology, seeing a celestial body like the sun or moon during certain times of day was associated with change and comfort in life related to health, love, career, and other material concerns. In some tribal cultures, this alignment was seen as an opportunity for renewal and hope after a period of misfortune. The sight of the two combined can be quite awe-inspiring and spiritual for many people around the world. It is a personal decision whether it's something interpreted through sacred texts or taken more symbolically.

5. Lunar Eclipse

Seeing a lunar eclipse has a variety of meanings. For Hindus, such an event holds immense significance and is believed to be highly inauspicious. It is considered an omen of bad luck and a foreshadowing of poverty, death, or destruction. This view can be traced back to the ancient Hindu texts known as the Shastras, which attributed these ideas to lunar eclipses. Similarly, in Jewish culture, it represents the same spiritual and portentous meaning, as an eclipse symbolizes a sign from God. The idea of cosmic prophecy through eclipses is also found in some Native American tribes, who tend to view it as a means of prognostication. Overall, lunar eclipses are steeped in religious tradition and superstition used by many cultures worldwide to explain this rare phenomenon.

Bird Omens

Blackbirds symbolize the balance between nature and humankind.
https://unsplash.com/photos/H6NaGPR1SX0?utm_source=unsplash&utm_medium=referral&utm_content=creditShareLink

1. Birds Pooping on Your Head

While a bird pooping on your head might not seem like the most ideal way to receive good luck, it is indeed considered an auspicious sign across many cultures. Spanning Christianity to Hinduism, the notion that a dove leaving its droppings on someone's head symbolizes financial and material success has been pervasive for centuries. It also signifies fertility. The origins of this "good luck omen" is said to have begun when Noah released a dove after 40 days of rain, and the bird eventually returned with an unexpected, blessed surprise. People then assumed that if they were fortunate enough to be "blessed" by a dove in such a way, their fortunes would surely follow suit. Although it certainly doesn't make it any less gross when you are actually experiencing this unique event, perhaps thinking about the long-standing good luck tradition may help.

2. Blackbird Making a Nest in Your House

In many cultures, the superstitious notion of a blackbird making its nest in your home is considered a sign of good luck. It is believed that such an occurrence symbolizes the protection of one's house, joy, fertility, and prosperity for those living there. In Celtic tradition, a blackbird taking residence was taken as a sign from spirit guides or deities that peace and harmony would be brought to the home. It was also thought to bring luck in financial endeavors. Similarly, Native Americans viewed the nesting of a blackbird as a symbol of balance between nature and humankind and believed it to be an opportunity to forge a closer relationship with Mother Nature. In Norse culture, the nesting of this species of bird was considered sacred and symbolic of guidance in life paths if observed by humans. These are but some examples that point to the great cultural significance this omen has held throughout history.

3. Seeing Five Crows Together

Beliefs and superstitions about crows have been around for centuries, probably because they are incredibly intelligent birds. A popular omen has been that sickness will follow if you spot five crows, and *death will follow* if you see six crows. This may be seen as a grim omen, but it also can be interpreted as a warning for people to pay attention to their environment and the signs of nature that surround them. The birds' behavior may provide warnings or clues about the unspoken danger lurking in the air, whether it's an impending illness or some other tumultuous energy from elsewhere in the area, so that people take action to protect themselves and their loved ones. While this particular superstition seems morbid, it serves an important purpose in many cultures and doesn't necessarily mean one should live life in fear of crows!

4. Spotting an Owl During Day

Seeing an owl during the day is widely considered to be a sign of bad luck or ill portent, with a varied and, at times, contradictory meaning depending on the culture. In Ancient Roman folklore, an owl signified death and would scream when struck by lightning, while ancient Greeks associated it with fertility and wisdom. Some Native American cultures saw owls as war-associated symbols, while in Africa, owls were thought to signify witchcraft. This nocturnal creature is commonly seen as a symbol of darkness and misfortune throughout many cultures, despite its more positive connotations in some mythologies. The origin of such beliefs has been a source of fascination for historians. Some people believe that such superstitions are linked to early human tendencies towards animism, while others attribute it to the silent flight and nighttime habits of this solitary predator.

5. Tip Your Hat if You See a Magpie

Have you ever heard the phrase "Tip your hat to a magpie?" It is a phrase rooted in a superstition that originated centuries ago. The superstition goes like this: supposedly, if someone sees a lone magpie, they should acknowledge it by tipping their hat or bowing to prevent bad luck from befalling them. This tradition has been popular in many cultures, such as Indian, Irish, and British. Its origin is thought to come from folklore, which tells how magpies symbolize mysterious prophecies and wisdom. It is hard to know for certain where this superstition came from, but it serves as an interesting reminder of how past cultural beliefs seep into our everyday lives.

Chapter 4: The Symbolism of Colors

Did you know that in some cultures, wearing a certain color on a specific day of the week is believed to bring good luck? For example, wearing yellow on a Monday in Thailand is believed to bring good fortune, while red is considered lucky on a Thursday in Mexico. Meanwhile, green is considered unlucky in some parts of India because it is associated with infidelity. In China, red is thought to bring good luck and is often used in celebrations like weddings and the Lunar New Year. Superstitions surrounding colors are everywhere, ranging from the common to the downright bizarre.

Colors can symbolize different things in different cultures.
https://pixabay.com/images/id-2468874/

But color superstitions aren't limited to clothing or personal items. In some cultures, even the colors of food have a significant meaning. For example, in Japan, eating black beans on the day of the Setsubun festival is believed to ward off evil spirits, while in many Western countries, eating black-eyed peas on New Year's Day is believed to bring good luck and prosperity for the year ahead. Whether you believe in the power of color superstitions or not, it's hard to deny their influence on our culture and traditions.

This chapter will explore the fascinating and often surprising world of color superstitions, from the common to the obscure, and discover how colors have shaped our beliefs and practices for centuries. So, let's take a journey through the rainbow and discover the intriguing and often amusing world of color superstitions.

Red

In many Eastern cultures, red is associated with luck, happiness, and prosperity. For example, in China, red is often used during important celebrations, such as the Lunar New Year and weddings, to symbolize good fortune and happiness. Similarly, in India, red is often used in traditional clothing and is associated with love, passion, and purity. In Western cultures, however, red often has more negative connotations. It can be associated with danger, passion, and anger and sometimes symbolizes warning or prohibition. For example, red is often used in stop signs and traffic signals to signify danger or the need to halt.

Red is also associated with love and Valentine's Day, with many people sending red roses or gifting red heart-shaped items to their significant others. Interestingly, red has also been associated with political and revolutionary movements throughout history. In the 20th century, the color red was adopted by socialist and communist movements, such as the Soviet Union and the Chinese Communist Party, to represent the struggle of the working class and the ideals of communism.

Superstitions:

- In Chinese culture, red is believed to bring good luck and ward off evil spirits, especially during the Lunar New Year. It is common for people to wear red clothing, hang red decorations, and give red envelopes filled with money during the holiday. Red is also believed to bring success and happiness in other areas of life, such as in business or relationships.

- In some African cultures, red is believed to have healing properties and is associated with blood and vitality. For example, wearing red clothing can help improve blood circulation and promote good health. Red is also thought to protect against evil spirits and negative energy.
- In many Western cultures, seeing a red bird, such as a cardinal, is meant to be good luck or even be a sign from a loved one who has passed away. Some people believe their wish will come true if they make a wish when they see a red bird. This belief may stem from the idea that red is a powerful and auspicious color.
- In some parts of Europe, red is associated with witchcraft and the devil. Witches were believed to wear red to indicate their allegiance to the devil, and red candles were used in their spells. Some cultures also believe that red is a color of warning and danger.
- On the flip side, in some cultures, seeing a red object or animal is believed to be a warning of danger or an impending disaster. For example, in Russia, seeing a red sky at night is believed to be a sign of bad weather, while in some parts of Africa, a red moon is considered a bad omen.
- Red is also commonly associated with love and passion, and wearing red clothing or using red in home decor can enhance romantic relationships and attract love. Some people believe giving red roses or other red flowers to a loved one is a powerful symbol of love and affection.
- In India, people believe wearing a red bindi (a decorative dot) on the forehead can protect a woman and bring good luck. The bindi is often worn by married women and is believed to represent the third eye and the power of intuition.

Green

Green has been associated with growth, renewal, and the natural world in many cultures throughout history. This association is likely since green is the color of plants and leaves, which are essential to life on Earth. In many cultures, green is seen as a symbol of new beginnings, regeneration, and hope. For example, in ancient Egyptian culture, the god Osiris was often depicted with green skin to symbolize his connection to rebirth and the life cycle. In Islamic culture, green is associated with paradise and is often used in architecture and design to represent new life and growth.

Green is also closely associated with the concept of fertility in terms of agriculture and human reproduction. In some cultures, green is considered to be a lucky color for weddings and is thought to bring good fortune to couples trying to conceive. Additionally, green is often associated with balance and harmony, perhaps because it is located in the middle of the visible color spectrum. In traditional Chinese medicine, for example, green is associated with the liver and is believed to promote balance and good health.

Superstitions:

- In some parts of Europe, wearing green on stage is bad luck for performers. This belief may come from the idea that green is associated with fairies and other supernatural creatures, which were believed to interfere with human activity.
- In Irish folklore, green is associated with good luck and is believed to bring wealth and prosperity. The green shamrock is the national symbol of Ireland and is associated with St. Patrick's Day, celebrated on March 17th.
- In some Asian cultures, green is also associated with fertility and is believed to bring good luck to couples trying to conceive. For example, in traditional Chinese medicine, green is associated with the liver, which is thought to be the organ that governs reproduction. Green jade is often used in jewelry and other decorative objects to promote fertility and good luck.
- In some African cultures, green is associated with nature and is believed to have protective properties. It is often used in rituals and ceremonies to ward off evil spirits and promote good health and wellbeing.

Blue

Blue is a color that is often associated with tranquility, wisdom, loyalty, spirituality, and masculinity. Across cultures, blue is frequently used to evoke a sense of calmness and peacefulness, such as the sky or the ocean. It is also associated with knowledge, intelligence, and wisdom, as well as with trust and loyalty in business and politics. Blue is also used in many religions to represent spiritual qualities, such as inner peace and devotion. Additionally, in some cultures, blue is associated with masculinity and strength, symbolizing qualities such as power and endurance. Overall, the color blue has diverse symbolic meanings that have persisted across cultures and time periods.

Superstitions:

- In many cultures, blue sapphires are thought to bring good luck and protect against harm. In medieval Europe, blue sapphires were believed to protect against poisoning and evil spirits, while in Hindu culture, they are associated with the planet Saturn and are believed to bring wisdom, clarity, and good fortune.
- **Blue Eye:** In some cultures, blue eyes are considered lucky or protective. For example, in Turkey and parts of the Middle East, it is believed that wearing a blue eye charm or "nazar" can protect against the "evil eye," a curse that is said to bring bad luck or harm.
- **Blue Flames:** In some cultures, blue flames are considered a bad omen associated with death and destruction. In Japan, blue flames are said to be the ghosts of the dead and are often seen at haunted locations. Similarly, in Hindu mythology, blue flames are thought to be the manifestation of the goddess Kali, who represents destruction and death.
- **Blue Butterflies:** In some Native American cultures, blue butterflies are considered a sign of good luck or a messenger from the spirit world. In Cherokee culture, blue butterflies are thought to bring messages of hope and guidance from ancestors or spirits. Similarly, in Chinese culture, blue butterflies are thought to symbolize love and joy and are often associated with the famous love story of the Butterfly Lovers.

White

White is thought to symbolize purity, innocence, and spirituality across many cultures. In many Western cultures, white is associated with weddings, representing purity and new beginnings. In contrast, in many Eastern cultures, white is often connected with death and mourning, as it represents the end of life and the transition to the afterlife. White is also linked to cleanliness and sterility and is often used in medical and scientific settings. In some cultures, white is believed to have healing properties and is associated with spiritual purification and enlightenment. For example, in Hinduism, the color white is associated with the god Vishnu and is used in religious ceremonies and rituals. Similarly, in Buddhism, white symbolizes the purity of the Buddha's teachings and is associated with inner peace and spiritual enlightenment. Overall, the color white holds a diverse range of symbolic meanings across different cultures.

Superstitions:

- **White Flowers:** In many Eastern cultures, giving someone white flowers, particularly white chrysanthemums, is considered to be a sign of bad luck and is associated with death and mourning. Similarly, some Western cultures often associate white lilies with funerals and are not given as gifts.
- **White Clothes:** In many cultures, wearing white clothes is believed to bring good luck and ward off evil spirits. In some parts of the world, white clothing is worn during religious ceremonies or rituals to represent purity and spiritual enlightenment. However, in some cultures, wearing white after Labor Day or before Memorial Day in the United States is considered bad luck.
- **White Animals:** In many cultures, white animals are considered to be sacred or special in some way. For example, in Hinduism, white cows are considered sacred and often worshiped. Similarly, in Native American cultures, white buffaloes symbolize peace and harmony, and their birth is seen as a sign of good fortune.
- **White Horses:** In some cultures, white horses are believed to be a sign of good luck and are associated with purity and spirituality. In Greek mythology, the god Apollo is often depicted riding a white horse, and in Hindu mythology, the god Vishnu is also often depicted riding a white horse.
- **White Owls:** In many cultures, white owls are associated with death and are believed to be harbingers of bad luck. In some Native American cultures, white owls are considered to be messengers of death, and their hooting is believed to signal the approach of a loved one's passing.

Black

Black is a color that has been associated with a range of meanings and symbolism throughout history and across cultures. In many cultures, black is associated with death and mourning and is often worn at funerals and other solemn occasions. In some parts of the world, black is also linked with evil, darkness, and the unknown. However, in some cultures, black is connected with power, strength, and elegance. In fashion, black is often seen as a classic and sophisticated color and is often worn in formal or professional settings. In some cultures, black is also associated with wisdom, knowledge, and experience, as seen in the traditional black robes worn by scholars and judges. Overall, the symbolism of black is complex and multifaceted, and its meaning can vary widely depending on the context and culture in which it is used. While it is often associated with negative or ominous symbolism, it can also be associated with positive and powerful symbolism as well.

Superstitions:

- **Black Cats:** In many cultures, black cats are associated with bad luck, witchcraft, and even death. It is believed that if a black cat crosses your path, it will bring you bad luck. In some cultures, however, black cats are seen as good luck, particularly in areas of England and Scotland.

- **Black Clothing:** In some cultures, wearing black clothing is associated with death and mourning and is often worn at funerals or other somber occasions. In other cultures, black clothing is associated with power and elegance and is often worn by wealthy or influential individuals.

- **Black Magic:** The term "black magic" is often used to describe dark or evil practices and is often associated with witchcraft, sorcery, and other supernatural practices. In some cultures, it is believed that black magic can bring about illness, misfortune, or even death.

- **Black Candles:** In some cultures, black candles are associated with negative or harmful energy and are often used in rituals or spells aimed at causing harm to others. In other cultures, black candles are associated with protection and the banishment of negative energy.

Purple

Purple is often associated with luxury, royalty, and power. This association likely stems from the rarity and expense of the dyes used to produce purple in ancient times. For example, in ancient Rome, purple was reserved for the clothing of the emperor and the highest-ranking officials. In addition to its association with power and status, purple is also sometimes associated with spirituality and mysticism. This is partly due to the fact that it is a less common color in nature and can be seen as otherworldly or ethereal. In some cultures, purple is also associated with creativity and artistic expression.

Superstitions:

- **Wearing Purple Clothing:** In some cultures, it is believed that wearing purple clothing can bring good luck or enhance psychic abilities. However, in other cultures, purple clothing is associated with mourning and is considered inappropriate for festive occasions.
- **Purple Flowers:** In some traditions, purple flowers are associated with spirituality and are often used in religious or ceremonial contexts. However, in other cultures, purple flowers are thought to bring bad luck or represent death and are avoided.
- **Purple Amethyst:** In some New Age and spiritual traditions, purple amethyst crystals have healing properties and can help enhance intuition and spiritual awareness.
- **Purple in Dreams:** In some dream interpretation traditions, purple is associated with wisdom, enlightenment, and spiritual growth. Seeing purple in a dream can be interpreted as a sign that the dreamer is on the right path and making progress toward their goals.

Yellow

Yellow is a bright and dynamic color that has a wide range of symbolic meanings across different cultures. One of the most common associations with yellow is that of sunshine and warmth. Just as the sun is often associated with life, energy, and growth, yellow symbolizes happiness, joy, and positivity. In many cultures, yellow represents the dawn of a new day or the beginning of a new cycle of life.

In addition to its association with sunshine, yellow is also often connected with creativity and intelligence. Many cultures believe that yellow can stimulate the mind and enhance mental clarity and focus. This is why you might see yellow used in educational settings or in advertising for products that are meant to boost cognitive function.

Superstitions:

- **Illness and Danger:** In many parts of Asia and Africa, yellow is associated with illness, danger, and death. Some cultures believe that wearing yellow clothes or using yellow objects can attract misfortune or bad luck.
- **Infidelity:** In Russia and some other Eastern European countries, giving someone yellow flowers is frowned upon because they are thought to represent infidelity. According to this superstition, yellow flowers are seen as a sign of betrayal, unfaithfulness, or disloyalty.
- **Good Luck:** Despite its negative connotations in some regions, yellow is also considered a lucky color in other cultures. In China, for example, yellow is associated with good fortune and is often used in decorations during the New Year.
- **Wealth and Prosperity**: In some parts of the world, such as Mexico and some African countries, yellow is associated with wealth and prosperity. Wearing yellow clothing or having yellow objects in the home is believed to bring good luck and financial success.
- **Spiritual Enlightenment:** In some spiritual traditions, such as Buddhism, yellow is seen as a symbol of wisdom, enlightenment, and insight. The color is thought to represent the light of the sun and the power of the intellect, making it an important symbol for spiritual seekers and teachers alike.

From the fiery passion of red to the lively excitement of yellow and from the soothing calm of blue to the purity of white, colors have held immense significance in cultures and societies worldwide for centuries. Superstitions associated with colors can be found in all corners of the world, and these beliefs often have deep roots in history and tradition. While some may dismiss superstitions about colors as irrational or unfounded, they continue to play an important role in shaping cultural practices and beliefs. Whether it's avoiding the color yellow in Russia or using red as a warning sign in Europe, colors have the power to evoke strong emotions and influence our thoughts and actions.

While it's sensible to approach superstitions with a critical eye, exploring the symbolism and beliefs associated with different colors can also be a fascinating way to learn about different cultures and their histories. Understanding the meanings and superstitions surrounding different colors can be a fun and enlightening experience.

Chapter 5: Omens about Animals and Plants

Since the beginning of time, omens about animals, insects, and plants have fascinated and held a special place in the human imagination. People from all backgrounds and belief systems are intrigued by the idea that seemingly mundane occurrences can be interpreted to convey powerful messages about the future. In many cultures, one has only to look at an animal crossing its path to understand if good or bad luck is likely to follow. For example, in some places, people believe that seeing a lizard scurry across your way bodes ill for your upcoming journey while spotting a cricket could indicate good fortune on its way. Similarly, many societies see daunting warnings from certain plants. An oft-cited example is discovering a blooming yew tree near one's home, which soon foretells death in the family. The intertwining of superstition and admiration regarding omens about animals and plants has been a part of every culture throughout recorded history and continues to captivate our minds today.

Omens about Animals

1. Cats

Cats have been linked to omens of all kinds. Cats can bring good or bad luck or both depending on the culture or circumstance! One example is the black cat superstition found in European folklore, which says that if a black cat crosses your path, it indicates an impending disaster. This belief originates in the Ancient Egyptians, who kept felines in their households as symbols of protection against evil forces, the opposite of what we believe about them today! However, some cultures view cats positively, such as the Japanese belief that a white cat brings longevity and good fortune. Whether a particular omen is positive or negative, one thing's for sure: cats sure make life more interesting!

2. Deer

Often viewed as a symbol of divine or spiritual power and knowledge, deer are powerful symbols in many cultures around the world. For instance, ancient Greek mythology has the story of the goddess Artemis and her relationships with deer. Artemis is associated with hunting, mysteries, and wild animals, being considered the protector of women in childbirth and an earthly embodiment of self-will. Interestingly, seeing a deer is considered a sign from Heavens that one should face their current problems gracefully and with dignity. This belief stretches across different cultures; however, it has its roots in Celtic lore which tells of a connection between the spirit world, humans, and nature, especially regarding sacred animals. Deer –gentle creatures by nature yet obviously strong enough to carry antlers for protection – became an example of being resilient regardless of hardships faced. However, some signs could point towards misfortune, such as if someone hears a roaring or bellowing sound from a stag, as this is thought to represent tragedy. Throughout different folklore, you can see how when faced with danger or fear, they often rely on stillness or running away rather than direct confrontation - two things we could all learn to do.

3. Dog

Omens and superstitions related to dogs are widespread in numerous cultures and have been for centuries. These omens and superstitions are often linked to these beloved animals' role in society. For example, in some Native American cultures, dreamcatchers were hung near areas where a dog might sleep or rest, as it was believed that dogs had the ability to influence dreams. Similarly, Chinese astrology considers dogs to be a symbol of loyalty and protection, with many families adopting a dog as a form of spiritual guardian. In Japanese folklore, seeing a black dog before starting an important endeavor is thought to bring good luck and success. On the flip side of this coin, there are also negative omens associated with dogs, such as when some believed that to hear hearing a dog bark on New Year's Eve could signal the death of someone within the house during the coming year. In Europe, it's taken as a bad omen if a dog crosses between two people– as it is thought that the couple will quarrel or, if they're engaged, their marriage will not happen. Some cultures around the world believe dogs can detect the presence of ghosts or supernatural forces. This can go back thousands of years, and one example is the Greek belief in Hecate, the goddess of terror and darkness. Even today, many people still adhere to these types of superstitions.

4. Fox

In Asian and Native American cultures, foxes are viewed as symbols of wisdom and cunning, while Europeans sometimes consider them more tricky and mischievous. One famous superstition about a fox is that the sighting of a red fox during the daytime is said to be an omen of ill fortune. It signifies bad news or an unexpected occurrence that could potentially lead to distress or misfortune. This belief dates back centuries, with some sources saying that it originated in Celtic folklore, while others link it to Chinese mythology and superstitions surrounding the legendary "nine-tailed fox" spirit. Additionally, some people believe that spotting a white fox at night is an omen of good luck or prosperity, so these omens can be good and bad, depending on the circumstances.

5. Rabbit

Rabbits have been associated with good luck, omens, and superstitions for centuries. In cultures worldwide, seeing a rabbit has always been considered auspicious. This is partly due to the animal's incredible reproductive rate. Rabbits reproduce easily and rapidly, making them a symbol of fertility and abundance. When you come across one in your path, it can indicate that happiness and fortune are coming your way. In many cultures like Korean, Vietnamese, and Native American belief systems, rabbits are also seen as having healing powers or compared to wise old grandmothers bringing positive energy into the home with their presence. Whether you see them as messengers of joy or spiritual healers, rabbits carry an unimaginable amount of power.

6. Snake

Over the centuries, snakes have been widely referenced in many cultures and religions. In various contexts, such as Christianity or Ancient Egypt, snakes have been seen as a positive or negative symbol of power, wisdom, and energy. The serpent is also thought to be an emblem of transformation. As far as superstitions go, some societies consider seeing a snake a lucky omen that may signify good fortune or success. On the other hand, other cultures believe that finding a snake will bring death and destruction, so it's natural to feel apprehensive when seeing one. Ultimately snakes are regarded as powerful symbols because they remind us of how powerful and instinctual we humans truly are and that, very much like the mysteries found in nature, we all possess an immense inner power that can be directed to something creative if properly managed.

Omens about Insects

1. Ants

The belief that ants are a sign of good luck is a common superstition worldwide. In many cultures, having an ant nest near your home is seen as a harbinger of good fortune and success. It is believed that if an ant enters the house and follows you, it means that something positive will happen soon. It is also said that if you come across three ants traveling together in the same direction, this indicates luck and wealth will follow.

The flip side to this belief is that being bitten by an ant can have negative consequences. It is a sign that arguments or quarrels may soon arise in one's life. This superstition holds strong in some parts of Asia, where being bitten by an ant carries the belief that discord or disagreements will surely enter one's life.

Ants are revered for their hard work and perseverance, characteristics highly prized by many cultures across the globe, and so they have become symbols of strength, resourcefulness, and resilience. These qualities also mean that when an individual sees ants moving about their home, it can symbolize progress in whatever project or goal they are working on at the time. Additionally, due to their large numbers, ants have become symbols of fertility and abundance throughout history. Thus, their presence near one's humble abode could indicate good things to come from all corners of life, whether it be financial prosperity or more children added to the family.

2. Butterfly

One of the most well-known omens and superstitions regarding butterflies is that they are often seen as messengers from the beyond, more specifically from lost loved ones. It is believed that when a butterfly lands on someone, it could be a sign that this person's relatives or other loved ones will soon pay them a visit. In Greek mythology, for example, the butterfly was strongly associated with the goddess Psyche, known to represent the soul or essence of life. According to legend, if a butterfly landed on someone in ancient Greece, it would symbolize their soul being blessed by the gods above and that their family would soon be reunited. This belief also extended to Japan, where during times of mourning, it was said that when a butterfly alighted upon one's shoulder, it was a sign that their ancestor had visited them to express their condolences or offer comfort. Native Americans also saw butterflies as spiritual messengers from the heavens and often held rituals to honor this creature's connection with nature and those who had passed on before us. In some tribes, such as the Hopi, girls were given butterflies to wear in their hair at special ceremonies, which were said to help protect them against bad luck or harm. They also believed that if a white butterfly came into your life, you should expect an important message very soon.

3. Dragonfly

Ancient civilizations have believed dragonflies were prophetic, with some cultures believing that seeing a dragonfly was an omen of good luck or a warning about imminent danger. In many Native American tribes, the dragonfly symbolizes transformation and enlightenment because of its association with swiftness and inspiration. For this reason, it is seen as a source of hope to aid in overcoming obstacles. Dragonflies are seen as messengers from the spirit world, and they often signify change or transformation, either physical or spiritual. Seeing multiple dragonflies can mean you are being told to keep an open mind and remain curious; finding a dead one traditionally means someone close to you is deceiving you or has gone astray. One famous omen associated with dragonflies is that they are directly connected with the Fair Ones, also known as fairies or sidhe (pronounced Shee). In this belief, dragonflies can be seen as reminders that the spirits of Nature watch over us and continuously strive to be part of our lives. As messengers from beyond, the dragonfly symbolizes both spiritual and physical transformation. It, therefore, carries a message of personal growth and transformation if it lands upon you or your property. Dragonflies are thought to help bring about a balance between humans and nature by reminding us of our responsibilities toward keeping our planet healthy. Such messages encourage us to reconnect with nature and enjoy its beauty while being mindful of actions that can be detrimental. Bright-colored winged miracles and dragonflies will usually appear where there is water nearby, symbolizing abundance and hope for greater things to come.

4. Ladybug

Ladybugs are a beloved insect the world over, and their presence has been associated with luck and good fortune for centuries. In Asia, ladybugs were believed to signify an impending birth or an impending marriage. The Chinese believed that if a ladybug landed on a person's hand, it would bring them luck in love. In Europe, many cultures considered ladybugs to be harbingers of good luck as well. It was said that if one were to appear on your property, it could signify a prosperous harvest or success in business endeavors. In the UK and Ireland, spotting seven ladybugs together was said to bring seven years of happiness. In some cultures, such as Native American tribes in North America, dreams featuring ladybugs were thought to be prophetic messages from their ancestors. Ladybugs were also seen as omens of protection from harm and evil spirits in many cultures around the world. Some people even believed that having a ladybug near your home could prevent bad luck altogether.

5. Spiders

Spiders have been objects of superstition and omens for centuries. For example, some cultures view seeing a spider as an omen that you will soon be visited by a friend who will bring you good news or shared knowledge. This is the symbolism of the spider's web, which reminds us that we are all connected and share nature's wisdom. Spiders were also seen as sacred animals in ancient times associated with the Goddess Athena, the Greek goddess of Wisdom. Indeed, many people believe that spiders are messengers of good luck. So if you spot a spider on your travels, take notice and don't be afraid. It may just be bringing positive news for you, especially regarding hearing from an old companion very soon.

6. Wasps

Wasps have been regarded as signs of danger and jealousy in many cultures throughout history. In Ancient Greece, the Greeks saw wasps as an omen of envy, believing that if one encountered a wasp, it meant that someone was jealous of them. If a person sees multiple wasps flying around their home, it could mean they are being watched by jealous eyes or surrounded by enemies who wish to harm them.

In Japan, superstition surrounds the belief that when a wasp enters your home, it means bad luck is coming and should be quickly removed from the premises. The belief is so strong that some Japanese people will even go out of their way to avoid killing a wasp if spotted in hopes of avoiding any negative repercussions.

In Native American culture, wasps are seen as symbols of wisdom and protection. It is believed that if a person is being attacked or threatened by another person or animal, they may call upon the power of the Wasp spirit guide to intervene and protect them. Other cultures believe that seeing a wasp could also be an omen of warning, indicating possible danger ahead.

Omens about Plants

Foxglove

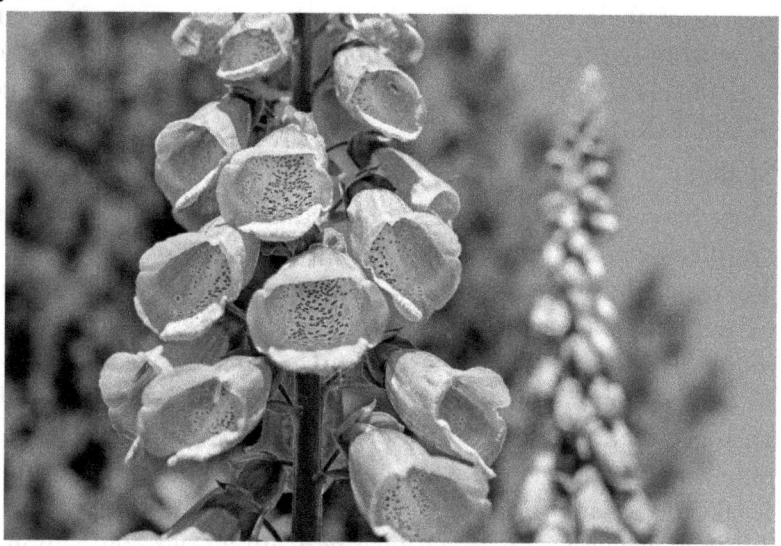

Foxglove plants can symbolize both good and bad omens.
https://pixabay.com/images/id-2372342/

In some cultures, foxglove plants are seen as being both good and bad omens. In some places, it is thought to bring luck and good health, while in other places, it can be thought to bring bad luck or even death. In Norse mythology, foxglove was said to have been used by Odin to scare away his enemies. He would wear a cape made of foxglove blooms while riding his eight-legged horse Sleipnir, across the night sky. This may explain why some people consider foxglove an omen of protection from danger or evil.

In Britain, there are several superstitions about foxgloves. One popular superstition is that if one were to walk around a ring of foxgloves three times, they would become invisible for a time. Another superstition is that carrying a piece of foxglove will make one immune from sickness or injury for a certain amount of time. It was also believed that carrying pieces of this plant with you when going into battle would protect you from harm and bring you victory in combat.

The Japanese also have their own beliefs about the foxglove plant. According to their folklore, stepping into a patch of the plant is believed to bring love and happiness in life. It is also said that if given as a gift, the giver will have luck in money and good fortune overall.

Fennel

The use of fennel as a way to ward off evil and bring protection dates back centuries. In ancient Rome and Greece, it was believed that the herb had magical properties which could protect against malicious forces. It was used in religious ceremonies and worn around the neck to ward off the "evil eye." Similarly, in Medieval Europe and parts of Asia, people believed that fennel could be used to keep away witches, demons, spirits, and other malevolent forces.

In India, fennel has long been associated with protective powers as well. It is traditional for Hindus to hang garlands of fennel over doorways to keep out evil forces and promote good luck. It is also believed that burning or using essential fennel oil can help purify a space or person from negative energy. People often burn bundles of dried fennel while reciting prayers or mantras for extra protection.

Folk medicine traditions across the world have long used this powerful herb for medicinal purposes. In Scotland during the 16th century, children were given tea made with dried fennel seeds before bedtime to help ward off nightmares and bad dreams. Similarly, Native Americans considered the plant sacred and would place sprigs of it on their heads or clothing to protect them from danger while they traveled through unknown lands.

Parsley

Parsley has a long history of being associated with superstitions and omens. It is believed that parsley was originally a gift from the devil himself. Some cultures think that the devil requires seven journeys between his realm and your garden before he will allow parsley to grow. Any seed that did not sprout was said to have been kept by him. This belief was so widespread that in 16th-century Europe, people would use their own blood as fertilizer for parsley to make it germinate more quickly.

This superstition has its roots deep in ancient European folklore and mythology. In Greco-Roman culture, parsley represented death and funerals due to its association with the Greek goddess Demeter's daughter, Persephone, who was kidnapped and taken to the underworld by Hades. Parsley also features heavily in many Christian rituals, where it is used as an offering or blessing during baptisms and other holy ceremonies. Parsley is also associated with love spells. A sprig of freshly picked parsley placed beneath one's pillow could allegedly bring good fortune in finding true love or help see into the future regarding relationships.

Rowan Trees

Rowan trees symbolize protection in Celtic Folklore.
Eeno11, CC BY-SA 3.0 <https://creativecommons.org/licenses/by-sa/3.0>, via Wikimedia Commons: https://commons.wikimedia.org/wiki/File:Rowan_tree_20081002b.jpg

Rowan trees have long been associated with superstition and omens. In Celtic folklore, the rowan is a symbol of protection, as it has protective powers that ward off evil spirits and bad luck. The symbolism behind the tree dates back centuries to ancient European culture, where people believed that planting rowan trees around their homes would protect them from malevolent forces. In Norse mythology, Odin was said to have hung nine sacred rowan twigs in the heavens, which formed a magical protective barrier against dark forces. In Scottish Gaelic folklore, the rowans are known as "fid na ndruad," meaning "the tree of druids." Druids were said to perform rituals beneath the shade of these sacred trees, and they were used as a way to invoke protection and blessings upon those who sought them. Additionally, rowans were often planted near doorways in Scotland and Ireland to keep out bad luck or malicious intent.

In Eastern European cultures such as Poland, Lithuania, Bulgaria, and Romania, planting a rowan tree outside of one's home is believed to bring health and happiness into the household. It is also thought that carrying an amulet made from a piece of rowan wood can bestow one with courage and strength in times of need. In England during medieval times, people believed that if you crossed your fingers when touching a Rowan branch, you would be granted invisibility for a short time, allowing you to become invisible and be safe from harm or danger.

Chapter 6: Lucky and Unlucky Numbers

Throughout history, humans have associated different meanings with different numbers. The concept of lucky and unlucky numbers has fascinated humans and has given birth to several cultural norms and practices. Let's explore these concepts in detail and determine how numbers influence our beliefs.

Numbers and Superstition

Numbers have a long association with superstition, with people believing specific numbers have particular effects or special powers. Some link seeing or using these numbers with good luck and fortune, whereas others connect these numbers to bad omens. Let's read about superstition and numbers in detail:

Lucky and Unlucky Numbers

Different cultures have particular numbers that are seen as lucky or unlucky. For example, in Western culture, the number seven is considered lucky because of the number's use in the Bible and the number's presence with cultural associations like the Seven Wonders of the World. The number seven also represents the colors of the rainbow. In contrast, 13 is considered unlucky because of its association with the Last Supper. This gruesome Biblical event records Judas Iscariot as the 13th guest, making the number seen as unlucky, especially from a religious perspective.

Likewise, in Asian cultures, the number eight is considered lucky because the sounds the number produces are similar to the word for prosperity. In contrast, the number four is considered unlucky because it sounds similar to death. These beliefs can often influence everything from business decisions to personal relationships.

Numerology

Numerology is the study of numbers which allows exploration of the mystical properties behind numbers. People with a strong belief in numerology advocate that particular numbers can reveal valuable insights into a person's personality and destiny. For example, number one is linked with leadership, the ability to delegate, originality, and independence, whereas number nine is linked to humanitarianism, spiritual growth, selflessness, and care for others. Numerologists use several different methods to calculate a person's life path number. According to their beliefs, this path number contains all the information regarding the person's traits and life purpose.

Astrology and Numerology

While numerology says numbers can reveal a lot about a person's destiny and life purpose, astrological studies advocate that the position of planets is a key influence on a person's destiny and life goals. For example, the position of planets in astrology determines the child's personality and destiny. Likewise, the numbers associated with a person's birth date can reveal their life goals and genuine personality. Here's an example from Western numerology. Specific numbers are associated with the letters of a person's name and added together to give a destiny number. This destiny number is believed to provide valuable insights into personality traits and reveal their strengths, weaknesses, and purpose.

Numerical Coincidences

People who strongly believe in the effects of numbers see several numerical coincidences as a sign of good or bad luck. For example, seeing the same number throughout the day or period can indicate a good or bad omen. For example, seeing the number seven on the clock or license plates more than usual can mean good things are coming your way. Some even firmly believe that the number of letters in a person's name or the numerical values linked with each letter substantially impact a person's traits, personality, and life goals.

In a nutshell, the link between superstition and numbers is complex and deeply ingrained in many cultures. While these beliefs may not be based on scientific evidence, they remain essential in many people's lives and beliefs.

Lucky Numbers

Lucky numbers are believed to bring good luck or fortune to those who use them. These numbers are based on cultural traditions, historical events associated with the number, or personal experiences. Many cultures have their own lucky numbers. While some cultures might see some numbers as lucky, other traditions can see the same number as drawing negative energies or indicating a bad omen. Below are some commonly used lucky numbers found in different cultures, beliefs, and traditions.

Number Seven

This number is considered lucky in many cultures. Seven is often associated with good fortune, completion or fullness, and spirituality. This number is widely used in many religions, including Christianity, Islam, and Judaism. The association of seven in religious traditions symbolizes perfection and completeness.

Number Eight

In Chinese tradition and culture, eight is considered the luckiest number. The sound the number eight produces when spoken in the Chinese language is similar to the sound of the word prosperity. Eight sounds like "Pa," whereas prosperity sounds like "Fa." This number is widely associated with wealth, success, and good fortune and is believed to have a pivotal role in business transactions.

Number Nine

Nine is seen as a lucky number in Japanese culture. The number nine in Japanese has a similar pronunciation to the word "longevity." This association of similar-sounding words and numbers gives the number nine a special place in Japanese society. The number is linked to happiness, longevity, good health, and bliss.

Number Three

Several cultures around the globe see the number three as a symbol of completeness, harmony, and unity. The number is widely expressed in art and literature and has a spiritual association.

Unlucky Numbers

Unlucky numbers are believed to bring bad luck or misfortune to those who use them. These can be based on cultural superstitions or historical events and are often avoided or skipped altogether. Some of the most common unlucky numbers include:

Four: Considered unlucky in many East Asian cultures, four is often associated with death, as it sounds similar to the word for "death" in many East Asian languages. This number is often skipped or avoided in buildings, phone numbers, and other contexts.

13: Considered unlucky in many Western cultures, 13 is often associated with bad luck and superstition. This number is sometimes known as the "unlucky" or "superstitious" number and is often avoided or skipped in many contexts, including buildings and hotels.

Six-six-six: 666 is considered an unlucky number in many cultures, as it is often associated with evil or the devil. This number is sometimes known as the "number of the beast" and is often avoided or skipped in many contexts.

In addition to these typical examples, many other lucky and unlucky numbers vary widely from culture to culture. Some cultures have different lucky and unlucky numbers for different occasions or events. For example, in some Indian traditions, the number nine is considered lucky for weddings, while the number eight is considered unlucky for funerals.

Overall, lucky and unlucky numbers are a fascinating and complex part of human culture, demonstrating the deep connections between numbers, culture, and superstition. While these beliefs may not be based on scientific evidence, they remain essential in many people's lives and beliefs. They are a testament to the enduring power of human superstition and tradition.

Folk Symbolism of Numbers

One: Unity, independence, individuality, beginnings, singularity. The number one is often associated with new beginnings and starting over. It represents independence and individuality, as it stands alone and is not divisible. It can also represent the singularity of the universe or a divine being. One can represent the self, leadership, confidence, and determination.

Two: Duality, balance, harmony, polarity, partnership, and opposition. The number two represents duality and polarity. It can represent the balance between opposing forces, such as light and dark, good and evil, or yin and yang. It also represents the concept of partnership and relationships. Two can represent harmony, cooperation, and diplomacy.

Three: Trinity, completion, perfection, spiritual awareness, creativity, and growth. The number three is often associated with completion, perfection, and the trinity in many religious contexts. It represents the unity of mind, body, and spirit. Three can represent creativity, growth, development, spiritual awareness, and connection.

Four: Stability, order, organization, the material world, the four elements, direction, and foundation. The number four represents stability and order in the material world. It represents the four elements (earth, air, fire, and water), the four seasons (spring, summer, fall, and winter), and the four directions (north, south, and east, west). Four can represent foundation, structure, and the importance of planning and organization.

Five: Adventure, change, flexibility, resourcefulness, versatility, and freedom. The number five represents change and transformation, the five senses, and the five fingers on a hand. It represents freedom, flexibility, and resourcefulness. Five can also represent adventure and the need for exploration.

Six: Harmony, balance, domesticity, family, community, love, and beauty. The number six represents harmony and balance in relationships, particularly in the context of family and community. It represents love, compassion, and empathy. Six can also represent beauty and aesthetics.

Seven: Mystery, intuition, spiritual awareness, analysis, wisdom, introspection. The number seven is often associated with mystery and spiritual awareness. It represents introspection, self-reflection, and the need for analysis and understanding. Seven is also associated with intuition and wisdom.

Eight: Abundance, success, infinity, material wealth, business, finances, power. The number eight is often associated with material wealth and success, particularly in the context of business and finances. It represents abundance, infinity, and the concept of power and control, and eight can also represent organization and management.

Nine: Enlightenment, completion, spirituality, universal love, humanitarianism, mysticism. The number nine represents completion and the end of a cycle. It is often associated with spiritual enlightenment and the concept of universal love. Nine can also represent humanitarianism and the need for compassion and empathy for others. It is associated with mysticism and the search for deeper meaning and understanding.

Ten: Completion, wholeness, achievement, accomplishment, integration, perfection. The number 10 represents completion and wholeness, particularly in achievement and accomplishment. It represents integrating and bringing together different parts to create a whole. Ten can also represent perfection and the search for excellence.

Number Thirteen and Superstitions

The number 13 is one of Western culture's most well-known and enduring superstitions and is associated with various superstitions and folk beliefs.

One of the most common superstitions surrounding the number 13 is that it is considered to be unlucky. The origins of this belief are partially clear, but there are several popular theories about its origins.

One theory is that the superstition surrounding the number 13 can be traced back to the Last Supper, where there were 13 people present, Jesus and his 12 disciples, and one of the disciples, Judas, later betrayed Jesus. This has led some to associate the number 13 with betrayal and view it as a symbol of bad luck and evil.

Another theory is that the superstition surrounding the number 13 concerns the Knights Templar. According to legend, on Friday the 13th of October in 1307, King Philip IV of France ordered the arrest and execution of all the Knights Templar, a powerful and wealthy religious order at the time. This event has been associated with bad luck and misfortune and may have contributed to the superstition surrounding the number 13.

In Western culture, several popular superstitions and folk beliefs are associated with the number 13. Here are a few examples:

Triskaidekaphobia is the fear of the number 13 and is one of the most well-known superstitions surrounding the number. Some people are so afraid of the number 13 that they will go out of their way to avoid it by avoiding travel, signing contracts, or making major decisions on the

13th of the month or on Friday the 13th.

Buildings without a 13th floor: Many buildings and hotels skip the 13th floor altogether, labeling it the 14th floor instead. This is done to avoid the superstition surrounding the number 13 and make the building or hotel more appealing to those afraid of the number.

Unlucky day: In Western culture, Friday the 13th is often considered the unluckiest day of the year. Many people believe bad things are more likely to happen on this day and will take extra precautions to avoid accidents or misfortune.

Unlucky in numerology: In numerology, the number 13 is often considered unlucky because it is seen as a combination of the numbers 1 and 3, which are both associated with bad luck in some cultures.

Lucky in some cultures: While the number 13 is often considered unlucky in most Western cultures, it is actually considered lucky in some other cultures. For example, in Italy, the number 13 is associated with good luck and prosperity and is often used in the lottery and other games of chance.

Overall, the superstitions and folk beliefs surrounding the number 13 are complex and varied and demonstrate the enduring power of human belief and superstition. While these beliefs may not be based on scientific evidence, they continue to play an essential role in many people's lives and beliefs and are a testament to the deep connections between numbers, culture, and superstition.

Spiritual Symbolism of Numbers

The spiritual symbolism behind numbers varies across different cultures and belief systems. In many spiritual traditions, numbers are believed to have deeper meanings beyond their mathematical value and are used to convey spiritual messages, truths, and wisdom. Here are a few examples:

One: In many spiritual traditions, number one represents the unity of all things and the universe's interconnectedness. It is seen as the source of all creation and represents the divine spark within each person.

Two: The number two represents duality and balance. It symbolizes the complementary forces of nature, such as yin and yang, light and dark, and masculine and feminine. In some spiritual traditions, the number two is also associated with partnership, cooperation, and harmony.

Three: Three is a powerful number in many spiritual traditions, representing balance and harmony. It is often seen as a trinity symbol, such as the Father, Son, and Holy Spirit in Christianity, or the three jewels of Buddhism (Buddha, Dharma, and Sangha). Three can also represent the past, present, and future, or the body, mind, and spirit.

Four: In many spiritual traditions, four represents stability and groundedness. It is associated with the four elements (earth, air, fire, and water), the four directions (north, south, east, and west), and the four seasons. In some spiritual traditions, four is also associated with materialism and the physical world.

Five: Five is often associated with the five senses, as well as the five elements (earth, air, fire, water, and ether or spirit). It is also seen as a symbol of balance, harmony, freedom, and adventure.

Six: Six is often associated with balance, harmony, and love. In some spiritual traditions, it represents the union of the divine masculine and feminine energies and symbolizes creativity and fertility.

Seven: Seven is a powerful number, representing spirituality, wisdom, and mystery. It is often associated with the seven chakras in Hinduism and Buddhism, the seven days of creation in Christianity, and the seven planets in ancient astrology.

Eight: In many spiritual traditions, eight is associated with abundance, prosperity, and success. It is often seen as a symbol of infinity and eternal life and is believed to bring good fortune and prosperity.

Nine: It is associated with spiritual enlightenment, transformation, and completion. It is seen as a symbol of the end of a cycle and the beginning of a new one and is believed to bring a sense of fulfillment and spiritual growth.

Overall, the spiritual symbolism behind numbers is complex and deeply rooted in many cultures and belief systems. While these beliefs may not be based on scientific evidence, they continue to provide meaning and guidance to many people on their spiritual journeys.

Beliefs about lucky and unlucky numbers vary greatly across cultures and regions, and what is considered lucky or unlucky in one culture may not be the same in another. That being said, here are some of the most commonly recognized lucky and unlucky numbers, along with associated superstitions:

Lucky Numbers

Seven: Seven is widely regarded as a lucky number in many cultures and is often associated with spiritualism and mysticism. In some belief systems, seven represents completeness or perfection, as in the seven days of creation in Judeo-Christian tradition. Seven is believed to be a lucky number in China because its pronunciation is similar to the Chinese word for "togetherness" or "union."

Eight: In Chinese culture, the number eight is considered extremely lucky because it sounds similar to the Chinese word for "prosperity" or "wealth." As a result, the number eight is often associated with financial success and good fortune.

Nine: In some cultures, the number nine is considered lucky because it is associated with a long life. In Chinese culture, the number nine is associated with the Emperor and is believed to be the luckiest number.

Unlucky Numbers

Thirteen: The number 13 is widely regarded as unlucky in Western cultures and is often associated with bad luck and even death. This superstition may have originated from the Christian belief that thirteen was unlucky because it was the number of people at the Last Supper (including Judas, who later betrayed Jesus).

Four: In many Asian cultures, the number four is considered extremely unlucky because its pronunciation is similar to the word for "death" in Chinese, Japanese, and Korean. As a result, many buildings in these cultures do not have four beliefs about lucky and unlucky numbers have been present in many cultures and traditions for centuries. These beliefs are often deeply rooted in superstition and not based on scientific evidence.

Lucky numbers vary from culture to culture. For instance, in Chinese culture, the number eight is considered lucky because its pronunciation sounds similar to the word for "wealth," while the number nine is considered lucky in Japan because it is associated with longevity. In Hinduism, the number 108 is considered very auspicious and sacred, while in the Western world, the number seven is often considered a lucky number, possibly because of its association with spiritual and mystical significance.

On the other hand, some numbers are considered unlucky in many cultures. The number 13 is the most well-known example of an unlucky number, especially in Western cultures. This is sometimes referred to as triskaidekaphobia. In many Asian cultures, the number four is unlucky because it sounds similar to "death." Similarly, the number nine is considered unlucky in Japan because it sounds similar to the word "suffering."

Superstitions associated with these numbers can range from avoiding using certain numbers or avoiding certain floors in buildings that contain those numbers to making important decisions based on a number's perceived luckiness or unluckiness. For example, some people may try to schedule important events on "lucky" days or avoid them on "unlucky" days, while others may avoid houses or buildings with certain numbers.

While these beliefs may not be based on scientific evidence, they continue to shape the way that people interact with the world around them, and the number four is often avoided at all costs.

Nine: While the number nine is considered lucky in some cultures, it is also considered unlucky in others. In Japan, the number nine is associated with suffering and misery and is often avoided. In Hinduism, the number nine is believed to be inauspicious because it is associated with the goddess Kali, often associated with death and destruction.

Overall, beliefs about lucky and unlucky numbers are deeply rooted in culture and tradition and can have a powerful impact on people's behavior and decision-making. While these beliefs may not be based on scientific evidence, they continue to shape the way that people interact with the world around them.

Chapter 7: Superstitions about Food and Objects

You are at your friend's house, and it is raining hard outside. As you are about to leave, you open your umbrella before you go out of the door. Suddenly, your friend gasped and exclaimed, "What did you do?" There is a common superstition that it is bad luck to open an umbrella indoors, as people believe that it brings misfortune. There are many similar superstitions, like walking under a ladder, breaking a mirror, pouring salt, or cutting a banana will also bring you bad luck.

Similarly, many superstitions are associated with good luck, like hanging a horseshoe in your home or eating black-eyed peas. This chapter will cover the most common superstitions about objects and food and their history and origin.

Food Superstitions

Every culture has its own food superstitions. Something acceptable in one country is considered bad luck in another. While some superstitions are related to history, others are derived from religious beliefs.

Bananas

Bananas symbolize freedom.
https://unsplash.com/photos/VI2rIoZUrks?utm_source=unsplash&utm_medium=referral&utm_content=creditShareLink

Bananas symbolize freedom, abundance, and generosity. Cutting this fruit up is believed to bring misfortune; instead, you should break it into pieces. Banana peels should always be thrown in the garbage; if one throws them on the ground, they can experience a terrible fate. It is common knowledge that slipping on a banana peel can cause serious injuries, which is how the superstition originated.

Seamen consider bananas to be a bad omen, so you shouldn't take one when you are on a boat or ship.

Black-Eyed Peas

Black-eyed peas symbolize good luck. Eating them on New Year's Eve in the USA will invite good health and prosperity into the coming year.

Bread

Bread is considered sacred in many countries worldwide, with some cultures even treating bakers as priests. Almost everybody eats bread, so there are various superstitions related to it that stem from many regions.

Baking Bread

According to a Scottish superstition, singing while baking bread is unlucky. Sometimes, after baking the bread, loaves get stuck together.

Count the stuck loves; if there are four, it means you or someone in your household will get married. However, if five loaves are stuck together, you will attend someone's funeral soon.

Bread and Butter

Dropping a slice of bread and butter on the floor can have a meaning, depending on how it lands. If it lands on the butter side, this means that a family member or a friend is coming to visit you, so you should prepare your home to receive guests. However, others believe that if it lands on the butter side, you will experience bad luck.

It is inspired by a Latin superstition that says if a child's bread falls on the butter side, it is a bad omen, but if it falls on the other side, it is good luck.

This superstition influenced the saying "Why does bread always fall buttered side down?" which one says to indicate the misfortune that befalls them after the bread falls on the butter side.

Cutting a Cross on the Bread

In medieval times, cutting crosses on loaves of bread could fend off evil spirits and protect you from witches. This superstition originated in England in the 1300s. A monk called St. Alban started this tradition and called it "Good Friday Buns."

Nowadays, in Britain, this superstition is still popular with people making bread and baked goods with crosses, but instead of making a cut on the bread, they draw it with frosting. Although people can make hot cross buns year-round, they are more common at Easter. In fact, people believed if you baked them on a Friday during Easter week, the bread would be enchanted.

Cutting the Bread

The way you cut your bread can either bring you good luck or bad luck. Cutting a loaf of bread evenly will bring you good fortune, prosperity, and success. However, if the bread pieces turn out uneven, it means you are lying about something or keeping a secret.

In another superstition, ancient cultures believed that cutting bread with a knife would bring you bad luck. Bread is a gift sent from God, so you should break it with your hands, as using a knife is an insult to the Lord. However, if you must use a knife, don't cut it from both sides. Cutting the bread from one side will bring you prosperity and blessings.

Finding a Corpse

Europeans and Indian Americans believed that one could use bread to find a drowned person. People would add quicksilver to bread, throw it in the water, and watch it float, and it would stop moving in the same spot where the dead body lay.

Last Piece of Bread

Never eat the last piece of bread, even if you are starving, as it will bring you bad luck. If you are unmarried and eat the last piece of bread before someone offers it to you, you remain single forever.

However, if someone offers it to you with butter on it, accept it and eat it right away, as it will bring you good luck, love, or money.

Making Your Mother-in-Law Love You

The Greeks believe that if you think your mother-in-law doesn't love you, eat the bottom part of a loaf of bread, and she will begin to like you.

Placing Bread Upside Down

Placing bread upside down can bring misfortune and invite the devil into your home. This superstition dates back to fifteenth-century France. At the time, King Charles VII held many public executions. He would ask ordinary people to act as executioners – so anyone holding an ax could get the job done. Many Parisians felt uncomfortable around the executioners; some even hated them. Bakers expressed their feelings towards them by making low-quality bread for them. When Kings Charles VII found out, he ordered that bakers must treat all their customers the same, *including executioners.*

Bakers decided instead of having to deal with these men on a daily basis, they would bake high-quality baguettes and place them upside down. This indicated that the loaves of bread were reserved for the executioners, and no one was allowed to take them. Executioners would walk into the bakeries every morning, take the upside-down bread without talking to anyone, and leave.

Nowadays, people believe that placing loaves of bread upside down will invite an equivalent to the executioner, like the devil or evil, to your home.

Rising Bread

If the bread rises while you are baking it, this indicates that a special person is thinking about you at this very moment.

Throwing Away Bread

Throwing away stale bread is considered bad luck – and even *sin* in some cultures. If you drop bread crumbs on the floor, it can also bring you a lack of prosperity. In Russia, they believe that after you die, the bread you throw away will be weighed in the afterlife to determine if you will end up in heaven or hell.

Throwing Bread in the Fire

According to ancient beliefs, if you throw pieces of bread into a fire, you will be feeding Lucifer. In another superstition, throwing it into a fire will lead to starvation. Ancient Catholics told children that Virgin Mary cried whenever they threw bread into a fire. For this reason, bakers cut a cross on the dough before placing it in the oven to protect it from the devil.

Eggs

Eggs represent fertility, hope, the cycle of life, and purity. If you use eggs and find one with double yolks, someone in your household will have twins. This superstition originated in ancient Rome. However, in Norse mythology, an egg with two yolks foretells someone's death.

In Asian cultures, eggs are a symbol of prosperity and good fortune.

Fish

Fish symbolize feelings, health, change, fertility, luck, and rebirth. In the Czech Republic, putting fish scales under your dinner dish on Christmas will bring you good fortune, and some people also put fish scales in their wallets to attract wealth.

Garlic

Garlic is highly regarded in different cultures because it symbolizes good fortune and can protect against dark magic. In ancient Italy, people believed that if you ate a clove of garlic first thing in the morning, you would experience good luck. While in Greece, people believe that the word "garlic" signifies good fortune and that hanging a head of garlic in your home will bring you good luck and ward off evil spirits.

In Poland, adults would eat a clove of garlic and utter the word snake in front of children to protect them from any back luck that a snake can bring them. One of the most popular superstitions related to garlic is that it can protect against vampires.

Grapes

Grapes symbolize abundance.
https://unsplash.com/photos/LYaW8eq3mjs?utm_source=unsplash&utm_medium=referral&utm_content=creditShareLink

Grapes symbolize variations and abundance. In Spain and South America, people believe that eating twelve grapes at midnight on New Year's Eve will predict whether you will have a good or bad year. Each grape represents a month of the coming year. A sweet grape indicates you will have a good month, while a sour grape indicates bad luck will befall you on this specific month.

Hot Peppers

If you are having a meal with a friend and they ask you to pass the hot peppers or jalapeños, place it on the table and ask them to pick it. Handing a friend hot peppers can cause trouble between the two of you.

Noodles

In China, noodles represent long life. Cutting noodles while you are making them will shorten your life. Try to eat your noodles by slurping them to ensure you will live a long life.

Onions

Onions are a symbol of unity, and in some cultures, they represent eternal life. It is believed that when you throw onion peels on the floor, you invite bad luck into your life and throw away good fortune. Hanging a small onion over your window will prevent evil spirits from entering your house.

Rice

Rice symbolizes good health, fertility, success, wealth, and prosperity. You have probably noticed that people throw rice at weddings. This is an old tradition that originated in Italy, and it is believed to bring fertility and prosperity to newlyweds.

In the Philippines, eating rice from the bottom of the pot will lead to a series of losses in your life. For instance, you will be the last person to get promoted at work, lose a race, and be last in everything in life.

Salt

Salt symbolizes preservation, purity, luxury, bad thoughts, and death. It is believed that spilling salt can bring you a string of bad luck. However, you can turn things around by throwing a small amount of salt over your left shoulder, as this is where the devil sits. This superstition originated from "The Last Supper Painting" by Leonardo da Vinci, where salt was spilled in front of Judas.

In ancient times, salt was very valuable and was used as currency. So when someone spilled it, they were wasting money, which is probably how it became a superstition.

Yogurt

Yogurt symbolizes transformation and gratitude. In India, people eat yogurt with sugar before getting into a new business, and students eat it before an exam to bring success and good luck.

Objects Superstitions

There are many fascinating superstitions from all over the world about different objects. Depending on your use, one object can bring both good and bad luck.

Horseshoes

Horseshoes have always been a symbol of good luck. However, a few superstitions related to them show they are more than a lucky charm.

Bad Luck

Hanging a horseshoe upside down can bring you misfortune, as luck will spill out. However, other superstitions say it can protect the house against the devil.

Fending Off Evil

Hanging a horseshoe in your home will ward off evil spirits and invite good fortune. Good luck can also extend to anyone who enters your house. In some cultures, if you hang a horseshoe on your door and have a visitor, they should enter and exit from the same door, or they will take all the luck with them. This superstition dates back to ancient England when the Devil came to a blacksmith and asked to make him a pair of shoes. The blacksmith recognized him and nailed a horseshoe to one of its hooves. The devil was extremely distressed and in pain, and the blacksmith took advantage of the situation, tied him up, and imprisoned him. He agreed to release him on one condition: promise never to step into a home if a horseshoe hangs on the door.

Under Your Pillow

On New Year's Eve, place a horseshoe under your pillow and sleep on it to invite good fortune into your life in the coming year.

Ladders

Ladders symbolize ascension, progression, and the connection between the physical world and heaven. Many cultures believe that walking under a ladder can bring bad luck into your life. This superstition originated in ancient Egypt. The ancient Egyptians believed that the pyramids and all other triangular figures were sacred and powerful forces of nature, and it was unlucky to break one.

A wall and a leaning ladder would make a triangle shape, so when you walk under a ladder, you are breaking the triangle, which is a force of nature. The ancient Egyptians also buried ladders with their dead, so they could use them to ascend to heaven. They also believed you risk annoying and angering the gods and goddesses when walking under a ladder.

However, it wasn't until the Middle Ages that the fear of walking under ladders became common. A ladder leaning against a wall looks a lot like the gallows. During executions, the people who were getting hanged would only get to the rope by climbing on a ladder. Before executions, criminals must also walk under one. People believed that if one walked under a ladder, one would one-day face execution. This is why people associate it with bad luck and even death.

Another version of superstition is associated with religion. The Holy Ghost, the Son, and the Father represent the Holy Trinity and the number three, which is sacred in Christianity. Since a ladder leaning against a wall looks like a triangle, walking under one can break the sacred Trinity. It is also believed to be a blasphemous act, a sin, and can invite the devil into your life. When leaned against a wall, a ladder can represent a crucifix which symbolizes death and betrayal, so walking under it will bring bad fortune into your life.

Mirrors

Mirrors are considered sacred in many cultures.
https://www.pexels.com/photo/oval-brown-framed-mirror-954539/

Mirrors symbolize vanity, arrogance, and water. In many cultures around the world, mirrors are considered enchanted and sacred.

A Good Scare

Sometimes, you can get startled when you walk into a place and get caught off guard by your reflection in a mirror. Although this may feel embarrassing, it will bring you good luck. However, don't try to startle yourself on purpose because it will not be effective. The scare needs to occur naturally.

Calming Your Nerves

Checking your reflection in the mirror when you are anxious or stressed will make you feel calmer and more relaxed. It is believed that the spirits will take all your problems away. However, looking in the mirror for a long time will provoke the spirits, and they can come for your soul.

Bloody Mary, Bloody Mary, Bloody Mary

One of the most popular and creepiest superstitions associated with mirrors is *Bloody Mary*. According to legend, when you light a candle and dim the lights, say "Bloody Mary" three times in front of a mirror, Mary will appear to you as a reflection. She will scream or grab you by the throat. She can even escape from the mirror and chase after you.

This superstition originated in ancient England when the queen of England, Mary Tudor, gave orders to kill 280 Protestants.

Covering the Mirror

Many people cover their mirrors after the death of a loved one. The belief is that spirits remain at their home until the body is buried. If the spirit sees a mirror, it will be trapped in it forever, and the mirror will take the person's appearance. This sounds like the plot of a scary movie.

Some people believe that mirrors are the devil's gateways and that they use them to enter this world. Covering the mirrors will protect you and your home from demons.

Giving Mirrors as Gifts

In Asian cultures, giving newlyweds a mirror as a gift on their wedding day is bad luck. Mirrors are easily broken, and marriage should be strong and last forever, and they can be seen as a bad omen when you give them as a gift.

Mirrors can also attract evil spirits, so they aren't an appropriate gift to anyone, let alone newlyweds.

Looking into the Mirror

If newlyweds look into a mirror together right after they get married, their souls will be united forever. They will also create an alternative reality where their souls will spend eternity together.

Seven Years of Bad Luck

In ancient Rome, breaking a mirror will bring you seven years of bad luck. They believed that life renewed itself every seven years, which is when the curse would end.

On the other hand, a mirror that doesn't break no matter how many times you drop it symbolizes good luck. However, this doesn't mean you should keep dropping a mirror to get good luck because once it breaks, your luck will change for the worse.

Umbrellas

Umbrellas symbolize femininity, shelter, power, prosperity, and protection. Many people worldwide believe that opening an umbrella indoors can bring them bad luck and unhappiness. The origin of this superstition goes back to ancient Egypt. The ancient Egyptians believed that opening umbrellas indoors was an offense to Ra, the god of the sun and the creator of the universe, so he was one of the most respected deities among his people. So when one offended him, they risked their anger and bad luck because they opened the umbrella away from the sun. Ra wouldn't just punish the person who opened the umbrella and all the people living in the house.

Some people believe that only a black umbrella or a new one will bring back luck if opened indoors. In modern times, people believe that opening an umbrella indoors isn't a good idea. It can invite ghosts and evil spirits into your home, bring discord between you and a loved one, and can also predict an impending death.

Superstitions about food and objects have been around for centuries. One object can bring both good luck and bad luck depending on the culture or how you use it. Some of these superstitions can even turn around the biggest disbelievers. For instance, eating a clove of garlic on an empty stomach doesn't only bring you good luck- it also prevents diseases. Opening an umbrella in your home won't only invite misfortune, but it can also damage your possessions.

Chapter 8: Superstitions about Birth and Death

Superstitions aren't just related to numbers, animals, objects, or food. Many others are related to birth and death. Many old midwives' tales about pregnancy and babies have created fascinating superstitions that are popular to this day. Although various superstitions predict death, a few are related to burial, dead bodies, and cemeteries. While this can sound morbid, these superstitions have intriguing and interesting folklore tales associated with them.

This chapter will cover all the different superstitions about birth and death and their history and origins.

Birth

Many birth superstitions from different cultures are related to childbirth, parenting, and child-rearing. Some can amaze you, others can scare you, and some can be strange. It is believed that many birth superstitions originated because of parents' confusion with childcare and giving birth.

Announcements

In Bulgaria, women only share the news of their pregnancy with their partners and refrain from announcing the news to anyone else for as long as they can out of fear of the jinx.

Blue Eyes

In Bulgaria, people believe bad luck will befall the child if someone with blue eyes looks at them. Getting rid of this curse would require the parents to wash the child's left foot and right eye twice a day for three days.

Daggers and Scissors

In China, pregnant women shouldn't keep scissors, needles, or any sharp objects near their beds because they represent cutting the umbilical cord, which can lead to an early pregnancy or birth defects. However, they can keep a dagger under their beds because it protects the unborn child from evil spirits.

Doctor Bear

There is a belief in Great Britain that if a baby sits on a bear's back, it will not get whooping cough.

Eating Fish

In Canada, people believe that if an expectant mother craves fish, she should eat it immediately; her baby will have a fish head if she doesn't satisfy her craving!

Eclipse

In India, it is unlucky for a pregnant woman to be exposed to an eclipse as it can cause deformities to the unborn child. During an eclipse, all windows and curtains should be closed to protect the pregnant mother from any rays of the eclipse.

First Steps

In Bulgaria, parents have a lovely tradition called "Proshtapulnik" that they believe will determine their child's future. They set the table in their home and place a few items on it that are related to different professions. For instance, they can add a ball (sports), a ruler (engineers), a small board (teacher), and a toy stethoscope (doctors). When the baby takes their first steps and chooses one of these items, it will be their career when they grow up.

Funerals

The Native Americans believed that expectant mothers should steer clear of funerals because this could lead to a miscarriage. They believed that pregnant women carrying a new life shouldn't be exposed to the end of life, as the unborn child will want to join the deceased and return to the spirit realm.

Jewish pregnant women also avoid funerals because they believe the deceased's spirit can get close to the unborn baby and cause them harm.

Jump over the Baby

Catholicism is widespread in Spain, and many are devoted to their religious belief, so some of their superstitions are related to their faith. One of their popular religious festivals is called Corpus Christi and is celebrated in June, where they perform something called "devil jumping." In Catholicism, all babies are born with the original sin. So, they perform the Castrillo de Murcia tradition during the festival, which is meant to save the baby from this sin. Someone wears a yellow and red suit to look like the devil or El Colacho. Babies who were born in the last twelve months are put on mattresses in the streets then the devil character jumps over the babies.

Some Catholic churches believe that this jump purifies newborn babies from original sin. It will also prevent evil spirits from harming them and guarantee they lead a life away from the devil's influence. Just as with any superstition, some people are against this tradition and find that it can endanger the baby's life.

Keep Babies Off the Ground

In Bali, Indonesia, newborns should be kept off the ground for about four months after they are born. Infants are sacred in Bali, so allowing them to touch the floor is considered blasphemy, as the earth can tarnish and ruin their pure souls. They are believed to be the divine spirits of their ancestors or reincarnations of their dead family members and should be treated with respect.

In Indonesian culture, the soul of a newborn baby isn't fully established yet, so if they touch the ground, this will interfere with the soul's development and its connection with the divine. Therefore, babies should be kept in their cribs. After three months, parents hold a ceremony for their toddler called "Nyabutan," where they cut the baby's hair, give them a name, and serve food to guests. They should also sprinkle holy water to appease the spirits. During this ceremony, infants are allowed to touch the ground for the first time.

Leis and Pregnant Mothers

Leis are necklaces made of flowers, which tourists in Hawaii usually wear. Although it is a fun tradition, it can be bad luck for pregnant mothers to wear them. The Hawaiians believe that women who are expecting a child shouldn't wear leis or any type of necklace. Necklaces resemble the umbilical cord, so when a mother wears one, the umbilical cord gets tied around the baby's neck and ends their life.

In Hawaii, people also believe that Lake Waiau is enchanted, so throwing a child's umbilical cord in it will guarantee that they will live a very long life.

No Celebrations

Nowadays, babies are celebrated before they are even born with ceremonies like baby showers or gender-reveal parties. However, in some places in Israel, these celebrations are frowned upon. Jewish families believe that any pre-birth festivities are unnecessary because you are celebrating an occasion that hasn't even happened yet, and you are rubbing your happiness in other people's faces which can invite evil and bad luck to the unborn child.

No Mirrors

The Greeks believe that mirrors can seize a newborn's soul and trap it forever. For this reason, babies should never see their reflections. Some Greek families cover their mirrors with blankets when there is a newborn in the house.

Other countries around the world believe in this superstition. There are many superstitions around mirrors in different cultures because people always find them intriguing.

Not Glowing

Pregnant mothers love it when people tell them they are glowing, except in Russia. Women there believe that these types of compliments are nothing but false flattery and can bring them evil and bad luck. If someone flatters a pregnant mother-to-be, she should wear a red thread as a bracelet for protection.

Rubbing the Belly

Although many pregnant women enjoy rubbing their bellies to show affection to their unborn child, in China, it can lead to giving birth to a child who will be spoiled.

Saliva

In the Philippines, various superstitions are derived from pagan traditions. People believe that babies experience something called *usog*, which is a feeling of distress that comes from being affected by an evil eye. This usually happens when someone pays them a compliment. Because of this curse, the child could suffer from various diseases like a fever. Parents usually ask their friends and families not to compliment their babies. Suppose the baby is so cute that people feel the urge to praise them. In that case, they should say the incantation "pwera usog" to indicate that their words are well-intentioned and to protect the baby from distress.

However, if the baby is cursed by the evil eye, the person who cast the hex should rub their saliva on the baby's shoulder, forehead, and chest.

Seven Days

In Egypt, families hold a traditional ceremony called "Sebou" seven days after the baby is born. It is similar to a baby shower with a celebration, food, and gifts for the newborn. During the ceremony, the baby is placed on a cloth on the ground, and the mother hops back and forth over them seven times. The purpose of this ceremony is to protect the child from evil. Salt is usually sprinkled on the new mother and all around the house to protect them from evil spirits.

Sumo Wrestlers

No one wants to make a baby cry, but in Japan, it is encouraged as it brings the baby good luck. They even have a saying in the country: "Crying babies grow faster." There is a popular annual festival called *Nakizumo*, where sumo wrestlers try to make babies cry. Parents usually look forward to this ceremony as it determines their babies' health and future. The ones who cry the loudest will have the most blessings when they grow up because their cries fend off bad spirits.

The Moon

There are many superstitions around a full moon, so it makes sense for pregnant women in some cultures to be wary of it. The Aztecs (an ancient culture in Mexico) believed that when a pregnant woman looked at the moon, her baby would be born with a cleft palate (a mouth deformity). When expectant mothers went out at night, they would wear something metallic to protect their eyes from the moon's rays.

Touching the Belly

In many cultures, friends and families enjoy holding a pregnant woman's belly as it shows excitement for the new baby. However, in Liberia, pregnant women are very protective over their wombs. They believe that anyone touching it will invite evil spirits to kidnap the unborn child. They save this honor only for the people they trust, like family members and close friends.

Ugly Baby

In Siberia, buying gifts for an unborn baby is considered an insult. After birth, people should also refrain from calling the baby cute or adorable and instead call them ugly because it brings them good luck.

Wedding

In many cultures, it is a faux pas to try and outshine a bride on her special day, but it is a bigger deal in China. If a pregnant woman is in the same room with a bride and a groom, their fortunes will clash, resulting in bad luck that will only affect the unborn child.

Death

Many people are terrified of death. Everyone knows they will die, but no one can ever know when or what will happen afterward. This mystery has led to many superstitions about death from different cultures worldwide.

Clocks

Families in Europe stop all the clocks after a person dies.
https://www.pexels.com/photo/wall-clock-at-5-50-707582/

In many European countries, after a person dies, their family stops all the clocks at the time of death. This ancient tradition symbolizes that time has stopped for the deceased person. In modern times, this tradition is a sign of respect for the departed.

Not following this tradition will bring bad luck to the entire family.

Day of the Dead

In Mexico, a famous festival called "The Day of the Dead" occurs on October 31st, the same day as Halloween. There are many superstitions surrounding this day dating back to Samhain and Paganism. Followers believe that on this day, the veil between the world of the dead and the world of the living is at its weakest, and the spirits of the dearly departed can cross over to the physical realm and visit their loved ones.

East

There is a reason many graves are positioned to face the east, and it is related to religious beliefs. Christians and Jews believe that the dead will rise from the east on judgment day. However, this tradition predates both religions. Ancient Pagans, who worshiped the sun, believed that the East represented the future and the promise of a new life, while the West was associated with endings. They buried their dead east to west to symbolize living a full life, and just like the sun rises every day, they will also rise again.

Feet First

In Victorian England, people removed the deceased's body from their home feet-first. This is meant to prevent the recently departed from looking back and invite someone else to join them in the afterlife. This is also why they used to cover the deceased eyelids with coins.

Flowers

For centuries, people all over the world have placed flowers over the graves of their loved ones. However, some cultures have different interpretations of this tradition. The ancient Romans believed that the spirits of the dead roam around in graveyards. So, they would plant flowers there to create a nice space where their loved ones would spend their eternity.

In Europe in the 1700s and 1800s, people believed that flowers would blossom over the graves if a person led an honorable life. However, if weeds surrounded the burial grounds, they were bad and dishonest people.

Gloves

Another superstition from the Victorian era is that pallbearers or anyone carrying a casket should wear gloves. People believed that the spirit of the dead could enter the bodies of the living through their hands and possess them.

During that time, people were preoccupied with death as there were many incurable diseases and resultant deaths. Christianity also teaches that the spirits leave the body after death. However, people at the time didn't know where the spirit went. They didn't know if the spirit stayed with the body or was free to possess others. Since people didn't have answers, they made up their own. This led to the belief that touching a casket can lead the spirit to possess you.

This superstition is still popular to this day.

Headstones

Do you know that headstones originated from a superstition? Muslims, Christians, and Jews believe that when the world ends, the dead will rise and face judgment for their sins. This was a common belief among Europeans in the 1500s. However, they were worried that the dead would rise too soon. This is when they came up with headstones and placed them over the deceased head to prevent them from rising before their time came. In some places in England, they place the headstone at the feet so the deceased can't get up and walk.

Healing Powers

In the US, people believe that dead bodies have healing powers. Standing next to one during a funeral can cure you of various diseases.

Hearses

In the United States and many other countries, people believe that if a hearse stops in front of a house, someone in this house will die. In Africa, it is believed that three people from the deceased family will die if a hearse stops three times.

New Shoes

In Victorian times, people refrained from wearing new clothes or shoes at a funeral as it showed disrespect and brought bad luck.

The Philippines

Filipino culture has many fascinating superstitions about death.

- If you sneeze at a funeral, it is an invitation for the deceased's spirit to visit your home. However, you can uninvite them by asking someone to pinch them.
- Walking on guava leaves after a funeral will prevent the dead from following you.

- Never look at your house during a funeral, or you will bring more death and bad luck to your family.
- Don't go home after a funeral. Stop at any place first, like a coffee shop or a gas station, to prevent the spirit from following you home.
- Don't attend more than one funeral on the same day, or you or one of your family members will die next.
- Make sure that your tears don't fall on the casket, or the deceased cannot cross over to the other world.
- Whisper your wishes into the deceased ear so they carry them to heaven.
- Sweeping your home after the death of a loved one will banish their spirit and bring death to other family members.
- Break a plate after someone dies to stop the cycle of death.
- The spirits of the dead usually come back and roam around their homes. Family members should bury their loved ones without shoes to prevent hearing their footsteps.
- Adults should dress in black at funerals, but children should wear red so they don't get sick during the funeral or have nightmares afterward.

Threes

You are probably familiar with this superstition; celebrities die in threes. For instance, David Bowie, Prince, and Alan Rickman all died in the first few months of 2016. The same happened with Michael Jackson, Farrah Fawcett, and Ed McMahon, who all died in June 2009. There are many more examples of three celebrities who died within days or weeks of each other. This superstition originated from old English folklore that three funerals took place within a short time frame.

Thunder

In England, and specifically among Catholics, a thunderstorm after a funeral is believed to mean the deceased has entered heaven. However, if thunder hits during a funeral, this isn't a good sign as it means the departed will suffer in the afterlife.

Tuck Your Thumbs

In Japan, you should always tuck your thumb when you walk near a cemetery. The thumb in Japanese is called the "parent finger," so by tucking your thumbs, you are protecting your loved ones. If you don't, you will bring death to one or both of your parents.

Whistling

While it isn't appropriate to whistle at a cemetery, it can have more serious consequences. In America and Europe, it is believed that whistling at graveyards can summon demons.

Yawning

Covering your mouth while yawning is more than just proper etiquette. This daily habit originated from superstition. At funerals during Victorian times, people put their hands on their mouths while yawning to prevent spirits from entering their bodies.

People from all over the world are fascinated with the magic of birth and the mystery of death. This has led to many superstitions related to the two. During ancient times, people didn't have the technology or science that exists today. They had to come up with their own answers for some of life and death's biggest questions. Many of these superstitions have lived on and are still practiced by many people to this day. There is a reason people still follow these superstitions in the modern world. They are harmless and can bring good luck and prevent misfortune. When protecting your unborn child and avoiding possession, it is better to be safe than sorry.

Chapter 9: Wishes, Luck, and Fixing Bad Luck

This chapter sets out several superstitious activities to make sure luck will always follow you and your wishes come true. From carrying charms, such as a rabbit's foot, to knocking on wood or crossing fingers to blowing your birthday candle out, there are many ways to ensure your wishes come true. The chapter also lists several ways to fix bad luck if you've had the misfortune of inviting it unwittingly into your life.

Luck-Bringing Superstitions

Knocking on Wood

This saying is used in many cultures across the world. However, its origins can be traced back to the Celts, who believed spirits live in trees. According to the ancient Celts knocking on trees could call on good spirits for protection and eliminate evil spirits. Since many objects around the house were made from wood, the custom was subsequently transferred to these objects.

Christian beliefs are also linked to the power of wooden objects, such as the crucifix. This idea originates from Britain, just as the one attached to the 19th-century children's game "Tiggy Touchwood." This game is very similar to the modern tag game, except in this game, players tag one another by touching a wooden object.

Blowing on a Fallen Eyelash

The tradition of blowing on a fallen eyelash comes from a 19th-century British folk tale. A person would place a fallen eyelash onto the back of their hand and toss it over their shoulder while making a wish. If the eyelash fell, their wish would be granted. However, their wish wouldn't come true if the eyelash stuck to their hand.

According to another version, the person should place the fallen eyelash on the tips of their nose, then try to blow it away. If they succeed, their wish will be granted.

There is also a belief that blowing on an eyelash can help you protect yourself from the devil or other evil influences. This idea comes from an ancient belief that the devil, evil spirits, and magicians collect human hair to gain power over people. Blowing away your eyelashes guarantees the devil can't get hold of it.

Lucky Pennies

According to an ancient Romanian belief, finding a coin is a sign of good luck. This idea stems from a time when metal was considered highly valuable, so finding a piece brought many benefits to the finder. Other versions associate finding coins with the gods, referring to them as gifts and signs of protection. The person who found a coin was said to be favored by the gods and was under their protection.

The custom was carried into British, and later American, beliefs, where pennies took the role of luck bringing coins. Be careful when encountering a lucky coin. A penny will only bring luck if you find it facing up. If you find it tails up, turn it over rather than pick it up and leave it for the next person to find. Otherwise, it will bring you bad luck.

Breaking a Wishbone

In Ancient Rome, the wishbone was seen as a symbol of luck. At first, it was discovering the wishbone during a feast that was considered lucky. Breaking the wishbone became a lucky tradition only after someone accidentally broke it while eating chicken. While breaking the chicken wishbone, the person coincidentally wished for something, and their wish came true. Nowadays, if you want to make your desires come true, you'll break the wishbone with someone else. As the bone snaps in two between your hands, the person who gets the longer piece of bone will have their wishes granted. If both parts are equal in length, both persons will have their wishes granted.

Fingers Crossed

The superstition of crossing your fingers for good luck hails from Pagan beliefs common in pre-Christian Western Europe. Initially, the practice involved two people. A person made a cross with their own index finger and the index finger of another person. This was believed to combine their spiritual energies to ward off malicious spirits, get their wishes granted or seal a pact between the two.

Later, people realized they could invite their good luck by crossing the index fingers on their own two hands. Ultimately, the custom of crossing the middle and index fingers on one single hand was born, which is how the practice is performed today.

Blowing Out a Birthday Candle

Blowing candles is related to an ancient superstition.
https://pixabay.com/images/id-1850982/

This custom is related to an ancient superstition that flames carry spiritual messages. In European folklore and magical practices, blowing a candle allowed the person to communicate with spiritual guides. According to the belief, if the candle flame is extinguished on the first try, the practitioner's message has been delivered. Similarly, if you blow out your birthday candles in one breath while making a silent wish, your wish will come true. However, it won't be granted if it takes several tries to blow out the candles or if you say the wish out loud.

Tucking Thumbs Inside a Cemetery

In Japan, there is an ancient custom of tucking in one's thumbs when one visits the graves of their loved ones. This practice is linked to the

Japanese word for "thumb," which is also translated as "parent finger." The finger represents a parent or family member you must protect from death. You can keep your parents or family members safe from evil spirits by tucking your thumbs in when in a cemetery.

Itchy Palms

In certain parts of Europe, and the Caribbean, an itchy right palm can indicate you're about to receive money. In contrast, if your left palm itches, it's a sign that you'll be out of money. These beliefs stem from the idea that a person's right hand holds active energy, which attracts money and good luck. While the left hand is said to carry passive energy, which deters money and good luck. In some cultures, the roles of the hands are reversed.

Throwing Broken Dishes on New Year's Eve

In Denmark, people often save the dishes they have broken throughout the year, only to throw them at the side of someone's home on New Year's Eve. They usually bring the dishes to the homes of family and friends and hurl them at their homes, wishing good luck to the recipients in the coming year.

In a more subdued version of this practice, children in Germany leave a pile of broken dishes on the doorsteps of their family, friends, and neighbors. This way, they can convey their good wishes without potentially causing damage to people's homes.

Sweeping Dirt Away from the Front Door

According to an ancient Chinese belief, good luck and benevolent spirits will enter your home through your front door. To ensure their homes will be blessed with good luck in the coming year, the Chinese sweep their homes by gathering dirt away from the front door. Sweeping dust away from the entrance also guarantees that none of the good luck that is already inside the home escapes when cleaning. If the collected debris is carried out from the house, it is done through the back door. They also avoid cleaning on the first two days of the New Year to prevent good luck from escaping.

Bird Droppings

Strange as it sounds, in Russia, bird droppings are a sign of good fortune. You'll get money if bird droppings land on you, your vehicle, or your home. And if several birds leave their droppings on your property, you'll probably get a significant amount of money. You might receive a sizable inheritance or win the lottery.

Spilling Water Behind Someone

According to Serbian folklore, spilling water behind a person's back is a sure way to bless them with good luck. It is believed that the fluidity of the moving water grants good luck to the person behind whom it lands when spilled. Serbians spill water behind friends and family facing challenging tasks, such as taking a test, traveling far away, heading for a job interview, etc.

Eating Legumes on New Year

In Argentina, people seek to bring luck to their lives throughout the coming year by eating beans on New Year's Eve. Some Argentinians prefer to eat beans on New Year's Day to secure good luck, and it's also said to help keep their jobs. In Hungary, people eat lentils for similar purposes on New Year's Day. According to the Hungarians, lentils attract wealth; the more you eat on the first day of the year, the more money you'll have throughout the year.

Accidentally Breaking Bottles

In Japan, accidentally breaking a bottle of alcohol is a sign of good luck. If you suddenly knock a bottle off the counter in a bar in Japan, people around you will cheer as they believe that you've invited good fortune to the place. On the other hand, breaking a bottle on purpose has the opposite effect.

Planting a Tree

In Switzerland and some parts of the Netherlands, newlyweds often plant a pine tree outside their house to invite good luck to their new life together. Planting trees after a wedding is also believed to grant fertility. Others use trees or tree symbols in their wedding ceremony, seeking to bless their union and have good luck and fortune throughout their marriage.

Fixing Bad Luck

Using Salt

Salt is believed to bring good luck.
https://unsplash.com/photos/4OfaTz6SdYs?utm_source=unsplash&utm_medium=referral&utm_content=creditShareLink

Using salt is believed to bring good luck in many cultures. Interestingly enough, this belief originates from the same source that says spilling salt is a bad omen. Throwing salt over one's left shoulder is said to bring good luck because it chases away the devil who stands on that side. While it's most effective after spilling salt, throwing salt can also overturn fortune in other circumstances. However, throwing salt over one's right shoulder attracts more bad luck, which you don't want.

Alternatively, you can sprinkle salt into the corners of your home (or on the windowsill) to ward off bad luck. You can also cleanse yourself from negative energies by taking a saltwater bath.

Handing a Broken Mirror

If you've broken a mirror and are worried about bad luck, be careful handling the pieces, as this will affect your fate. For example, throwing the pieces away seals the "Seven years of bad luck" curse. Instead, take the fragments and store them away until the next full moon. When it arrives, use a piece of the broken mirror to reflect the moon and gaze into the reflection. In many cultures and magical practices, it is believed that the moon can nullify bad energies. By staring into it through the mirror, you can reflect on the positive things in your life. When you're done, bury the mirror pieces.

Using Incense or Herbs

In ancient herb lore, burning herbs is said to ward off negative influences responsible for bad luck. In modern times, you can achieve the same effects with incense, and this is especially true if you use an herb with an intense smell, like jasmine or sandalwood. If poor luck affects your personal life, burn incense at home by carrying it from one room to another.

Or, if you decide to go the traditional route, you can always burn sage. This herb has the most potent purifying effects and is guaranteed to help you turn your energies and luck around. Burning sage is also known as smudging, but you can use other herbs too. When you burn them, open your windows and doors so the negative energy can leave, and it will be replaced with a positive force and attract plenty of good luck.

Carry Protective Charms

Protective charms are fantastic tools for warding off bad luck. You can carry them with you as you go about your daily life, and they will always protect you from negative influences. Even if you're already affected by bad luck, wearing a small charm on a chain or bracelet or carrying it around in a pocket can eliminate its effects. Here are some of the popular protective charms used by different cultures:

- **Four-leaved clover**: Wearing a charm in this shape is a great way to attract good luck. According to ancient lore, each leaf represents a lucky aspect of life, bringing love, wealth, health, and fame.
- **Keys:** Key charms have been used to invite good fortune since ancient times. To improve your chances of replacing poor luck with good, it's best to wear three keys, which will unlock the three doors of wealth, love, and health.
- **Horseshoe:** According to several ancient belief systems, horseshoe charms can ward off the "evil eye." Wear it on a chain with its ends pointed upwards. Otherwise, good luck will stay away from you.
- **Rabbit foot:** A rabbit's left hind foot is also believed to invite good fortune and wealth. Others suggest it can also protect you

from bad luck. You can also wear it on your key chain; you'll just have to remember to rub the charm regularly to activate its powers of bringing good luck.

- **Crystals and stones:** Their magical properties are used in different practices. Crystals and stones can provide protection and healing and bring positive energies. They're believed to have their own powers, which can amplify the ones in and near your body. You can wear them as charms or use them as decorations at home or at your workplace. Some of the most commonly recommended crystals for warding off bad luck are black tourmaline, labradorite, and amethyst. Rose quartz can help you replace the negative influences with positive energies and good luck.

Engage in Charity

In many cultures, it is believed that the easiest way to invite good luck into your life is by doing good deeds. According to Buddhism and other Asian religions, you can repay any negative actions you have done by engaging in charitable pursuits. This is related to the concept of karma, which is a term these religions use for luck. Whether you donate to charity or help those in need in your environment, it doesn't matter. What matters is doing it altruistically and not just to earn good karma. Not to mention that engaging in charity can help you place things into a different perspective. What seems like poor luck to you can become a lesser issue when compared to the misfortunes other people face in their day-to-day lives.

Unblocking Your Chakras

In many Asian cultures, the chakra system is connected not only to one's health but also to one's luck. By cleansing them, you can remove the block that hinders positive energy flow inside your body. You can purify your chakras with colorful flowers charged with the sun's positive energy. You can display the flowers on your table or use them in your bathwater to let them soak up the bad energy inside your body. Throwing the flower away afterward helps eliminate these influences symbolically.

Encourage Spiritual Growth

If you're a spiritual seeker, you can also turn bad luck into good by promoting your own spiritual growth. You can do this by obtaining a level of spirituality that enables you to invite good fortune back into your life. In many religions, people pray to deities, spiritual animals, or ancestral spirits to improve their lives. While in other belief systems, gaining self-awareness is customary as part of a spiritually enlightening process.

If spiritual practices aren't for you, you can use self-reflection exercises and mindfulness techniques to learn which steps to take to better your luck. Positive affirmations and mantras can also help you invite good luck and chase away the bad ones. The more you repeat them, the more likely you'll be able to repel negative influences.

Clean or Declutter Your Home

Decluttering or cleaning your home can help you eliminate negative energies that prevent the flow of good fortune. It's a simple practice that can empower you to make the change you need to fix your bad luck.

There are several beliefs attached to superstition. One of the most famous originates from South America, where people have a specific way of cleaning their homes. Young women need to learn how to clean their homes properly. Otherwise, they won't find a husband or will have bad luck even if they marry. To avoid this, they're encouraged to sweep when no one is around, so they can avoid going over anyone's feet with the broom, which is a bad omen. If one gets their feet swept over, they must spit on the broom to avoid misfortune.

In other cultures, it is believed the furniture in a home or workplace should be arranged in a certain way to encourage positive energy flow. To help this energy bring you more luck, clear away anything standing in its way, including unused items, cobwebs, and anything else that creates clutter.

Some also believe that the sun brings positive energy and good luck. This idea is associated with ancient beliefs revolving around sun deities who brought new life and fortune to people by reviving nature during spring. Even opening the window and letting sunshine surround your home can help improve your luck and fortune.

Alternatively, you can introduce bright light into your space by lighting large candles or having a wood-burning fireplace. The larger the area illuminated by the light sources, the less room there will be for bad luck to hide.

Have a Change of Air

Traveling to another country is supposed to help dispel bad luck in many cultures. In ancient times, people often noticed that their poor luck stopped following them when they moved to another place. Or, even if they returned, the negative energies had dispersed, and their fortune turned for the better.

Nowadays, it's said that to get rid of bad luck, you must cross an ocean or travel to a country with different time zones. However, you don't necessarily have to go this far. Sometimes even leaving your home and workplace for a couple of days to take a trip on an extended weekend can do the trick. Sometimes all it needs is taking some time to understand what you need to change your luck.

Avoiding Situations That Attract Bad Luck

Whether you're still fending off bad luck or don't want to attract it, aim to avoid behavior and circumstances that could invite misfortune into your life. Try to behave in a way that helps you avoid bad luck. For example, you can be extra careful not to break mirrors, walk under ladders, put your shoes on the table, "jinxing" yourself, step on a crack on the sidewalk, or open your umbrella indoors. Or in other words, you should avoid inviting other bad omens mentioned in the previous chapters.

It's also a good idea to familiarize yourself with some of the lesser-known superstitions (such as picking up a penny with the wrong side up) and other beliefs you might not be familiar with.

Recognize the Signs of Good Luck

In many cultures, a small amount of good luck is believed to attract more good fortune. So, once you see the signs that your luck is turning from bad to good, try to pursue actions that can help you keep the positive flow going. Stay alert to recognize the signs and act in time.

Glossary of Superstitions, Signs, and Omens

1. Acorn

It is believed that carrying an acorn in your pocket can bring good luck and protect against illness. Some people also believe placing an acorn on a windowsill can prevent lightning strikes.

2. Apple

If you cut an apple in half and count the number of seeds inside, that will tell you how many children you will have. Apples are also sometimes used in divination, where the way the apple core falls after it is cut can reveal information about the future.

3. Bat

Bats are seen as a sign of impending doom and are associated with vampires and other supernatural beings. In some traditions, it is believed that if a bat flies into your home, it is a sign that someone in the household will die.

4. Black Cat

Black cats are considered to be bad luck, and people believe they can cause illness or misfortune. Some believe that if a black cat crosses your path, it is a sign that you should turn back or change your plans.

5. Bluebird

It is said that if you see a bluebird, it is a sign of good luck and happiness. Some people also believe that if a bluebird flies into your home, it is a sign of good fortune and that you will soon receive good news.

6. Blue Moon

A blue moon is the second full moon in a calendar month, which occurs only once every few years. Some people believe that a blue moon is a powerful time for magic and manifestation and that wishes made under a blue moon are more likely to come true.

7. Broken Mirror

It is said that if you break a mirror, you will have seven years of bad luck, and some people believe that it can also release evil spirits into the world. To ward off bad luck after breaking a mirror, it's suggested that you bury the broken pieces in the ground.

8. Cherry Blossoms

Cherry blossoms are often associated with beauty and transience and are sometimes seen as a symbol of the fleeting nature of life. Some cultures believe if you see a cherry blossom in your dream, it is a sign of good luck and love.

9. Chinese Coins

In Feng Shui, Chinese coins are often used as a symbol of wealth and prosperity. It is believed that carrying Chinese coins in your wallet or purse can attract financial abundance and good fortune. Believers also suggest hanging Chinese coins on the doorknob of your home or office to invite prosperity into your life.

10. Chimney Sweep

In some traditions, encountering a chimney sweep is believed to be a sign of good luck. It is said that if you shake hands with a chimney sweep, or if a chimney sweep touches your shoulder, it will bring good fortune and ward off bad luck.

11. Clocks

In some cultures, giving a clock as a gift is considered bad luck, as it is believed to symbolize the ticking away of time and approaching death. Some people also believe that stopping a clock can bring bad luck.

12. Clover

The four-leaf clover is often seen as a symbol of good luck and is sometimes associated with St. Patrick's Day. Finding a four-leaf clover can bring good fortune, and carrying one in your pocket can attract wealth and success.

13. Crossed Knives

In some traditions, crossing two knives is considered bad luck, as it is believed to represent a potential conflict or argument. It is also said that if you accidentally cross your own knives while setting the table, you should quickly uncross them and make a wish to avoid bad luck.

14. Crossed Legs

Crossing your legs is sometimes seen as a sign of bad luck or disrespect, especially in certain cultures. In some traditions, it is believed that crossing your legs while sitting in a church or a temple brings bad luck and is disrespectful to the gods.

15. Crows on a Fence

In some cultures, seeing three crows sitting together on a fence is a sign of impending death or disaster. This superstition is sometimes referred to as "three on a match" and is thought to have originated from the belief that lighting three cigarettes from the same match was bad luck for soldiers during wartime.

16. Dandelion

In some cultures, blowing on a dandelion is believed to make a wish come true. It is also said that if you can blow off all the dandelion seeds with one breath, your wish will be granted.

17. Double Yolk Egg

Finding a double-yolked egg is considered a sign of good luck and prosperity. It is also sometimes seen as a sign of fertility and can be a good omen for those trying to conceive.

18. Dreamcatcher

Dreamcatchers are often used as a protective talisman to ward off bad dreams and nightmares. The dreamcatcher traps bad dreams in its web while allowing good dreams to pass through and reach the sleeper.

19. Eclipse

Eclipses have been seen as omens of change and transformation throughout history. Some cultures believe the appearance of a solar or lunar eclipse is a sign of impending disaster or war, while in others, it is seen as a symbol of good luck and renewal.

20. Friday the 13th

Friday the 13th is often seen as an unlucky day in Western cultures. Some people believe this superstition dates back to the Last Supper, where there were 13 people present, including Jesus and Judas. Others believe that it is related to the arrest and crucifixion of the Knights Templar on Friday the 13th in 1307.

21. Goldfish

Goldfish are often associated with good luck and prosperity. Some cultures believe that keeping goldfish in the home can bring good luck and positive energy.

22. Grasshopper

In some traditions, grasshoppers are seen as symbols of good luck and abundance. It is said that if a grasshopper lands on you, it is a sign of good luck and success.

23. Hamsa

The hamsa is a symbol of protection and good luck in many cultures. It is often used as a talisman to ward off the evil eye and negative energy. The hamsa is a hand-shaped symbol, with an eye in the center, and is often worn as jewelry or hung in the home.

24. Horseshoe

Horseshoes are often used as symbols of good luck and protection. It is believed that if a horseshoe is hung over a doorway with the ends pointing up, it will catch and hold good luck. If the horseshoe is hung with the ends pointing down, however, it is said that the luck will fall out.

25. Knocking on Wood

Knocking on wood is a superstitious act that is believed to ward off bad luck or jinxes. It is often done after making a statement of good luck or success in order to prevent anything negative from happening.

26. Ladder

In a lot of European cultures, walking under a ladder is considered to be bad luck. It is said to bring about misfortune and is to be avoided whenever possible.

27. Ladybug

Ladybugs are often seen as symbols of good luck and protection. It is believed that if a ladybug lands on you, it will bring you good luck and happiness. Ladybugs are also used as natural pest control, as they eat aphids and other harmful insects.

28. Leprechaun

In Irish folklore, leprechauns are mischievous fairies known for their elusive nature and ability to grant wishes. They are often associated with good luck and are said to have a pot of gold at the end of a rainbow.

29. Lightning

Lightning is often associated with danger and destruction. In many cultures, it is believed to be a sign of divine wrath or a warning of impending disaster.

30. Magpie

Magpies are often seen as symbols of good luck and protection, particularly in British and Irish folklore. If you see a magpie, you should salute it and say "Good morning, Mr. Magpie" to ward off bad luck.

31. Mirror Gazing

Looking into a mirror for an extended period is believed to bring bad luck or even summon spirits in several belief systems. It is also believed that breaking a mirror can bring seven years of bad luck.

32. New Moon

The new moon is often associated with new beginnings and fresh starts. In some cultures, it is believed that making a wish on the new moon will make it come true.

33. Pennies

Pennies are often associated with good luck and prosperity. In some cultures, it is believed that finding a penny on the ground is a sign of good luck and should be picked up and kept for good fortune.

34. Rabbit's Foot

In many cultures, a rabbit's foot is considered a good luck charm. Carrying a rabbit's foot is believed to bring good fortune and protect against bad luck.

35. Red Cardinal

A red cardinal is believed to be a messenger from a loved one who has passed away and is seen as a sign of good luck and a harbinger of positive things to come.

36. Red String

In some Eastern cultures, the red string is believed to have protective properties. It is often worn as a bracelet or necklace to ward off evil spirits and bring good luck.

37. Shooting Star

Many cultures believe that making a wish on a shooting star will make it come true. Shooting stars are seen as magical and rare and are often associated with good luck and positive change.

38. Silver

Silver is associated with purity and is believed to have protective properties. In many cultures, it is believed that wearing silver jewelry or carrying a silver object can ward off evil spirits and bring good luck.

39. Thirteen

In many cultures, the number 13 is considered unlucky. It is believed to bring bad luck, especially on Friday the 13th, which is considered an unlucky day in Western cultures.

40. Thunder

Thunder is believed to be a sign of anger from the gods or the spirits. It is often seen as an omen of bad luck, and some believe it is a warning of impending danger.

41. Toad

In some cultures, toads are associated with witchcraft and magic. It is often said that touching a toad can bring good luck or grant wishes.

42. Umbrella

In many cultures, it is believed that opening an umbrella indoors is bad luck. It is also said that leaving an umbrella open will bring bad luck to the entire house.

43. Vulture

Vultures are seen as symbols of death and decay. Seeing a vulture is often said to be a bad omen and a sign of impending danger or misfortune.

44. White Butterfly

Seeing a white butterfly is believed to bring good luck and is considered a positive omen. It is said that if a white butterfly lands on you, it is a sign of good luck and prosperity. And, if a white butterfly enters your home, it is a sign that someone who has passed away is watching over you.

45. Wishbone

It is believed that if two people pull on the wishbone of a turkey or chicken and it breaks evenly, both people will have their wishes come true. It is believed that the person who gets the larger piece of the wishbone will have good luck, and their wishes will be granted.

This chapter provides a helpful quick-glance guide to the many common superstitions people still believe in today. By understanding the origins and meanings of these superstitions, we gain insight into the cultural and psychological factors that continue to influence our beliefs and behaviors. While it is important to acknowledge the significance of superstitions in shaping our worldviews, it is also important to approach them with a critical eye. By separating fact from fiction and relying on evidence-based knowledge, you can avoid falling prey to superstitions that may lead us down harmful paths.

Conclusion

This book has been a fascinating and thought-provoking journey exploring how superstitions have shaped our world and continue to influence our daily lives. From the common superstitions we all know to the lesser-known beliefs still prevalent in certain cultures, this book is a detailed look at the history and psychology behind these fascinating phenomena. Throughout its pages, you've explored the many reasons people believe in superstitions, from a need for control to a desire for comfort and protection. You now also know how superstitions have influenced everything from religion and culture to science and medicine.

As you reflect on what you have learned, remember that superstitions can have both positive and negative effects. While they may offer comfort and a sense of security, they can also lead to irrational thinking and harmful behaviors. It is up to us as individuals to approach them critically and question the validity of our beliefs. In the end, the power of superstitions lies in our ability to control our own thoughts and actions. By understanding the psychology behind superstitions, we can learn to recognize and challenge them when necessary and embrace them when they serve a positive purpose in our lives.

Superstitions are constantly evolving and changing over time. While some may have been popular in the past, they may not be as widely held today. Likewise, new superstitions emerge due to changing social and cultural contexts. Embracing the diversity of superstitions can be a creative and fun way to explore different cultures and perspectives. By learning about the superstitions of other cultures and communities, you can gain a deeper understanding of their worldviews and values and even incorporate some of these beliefs into your own lives. Whether carrying a lucky charm, avoiding certain colors or numbers, or performing a specific ritual, exploring superstitions can add fun and curiosity to your daily lives.

"Superstition is foolish, childish, primitive, and irrational - but how much does it cost you to knock on wood?" - Judith Viorst

This humorous quote by Judith Viorst highlights the contradictions and complexities of superstitions. While they may seem illogical or even silly at times, many of us still engage in them as a way to protect ourselves from harm or bring good luck. So, as you close the book on superstitions, maintain a balanced and curious perspective. While it's important to approach superstitions with a healthy dose of skepticism, acknowledge their emotional and cultural significance for people, and always be sensible.

Here's another book by Mari Silva that you might like

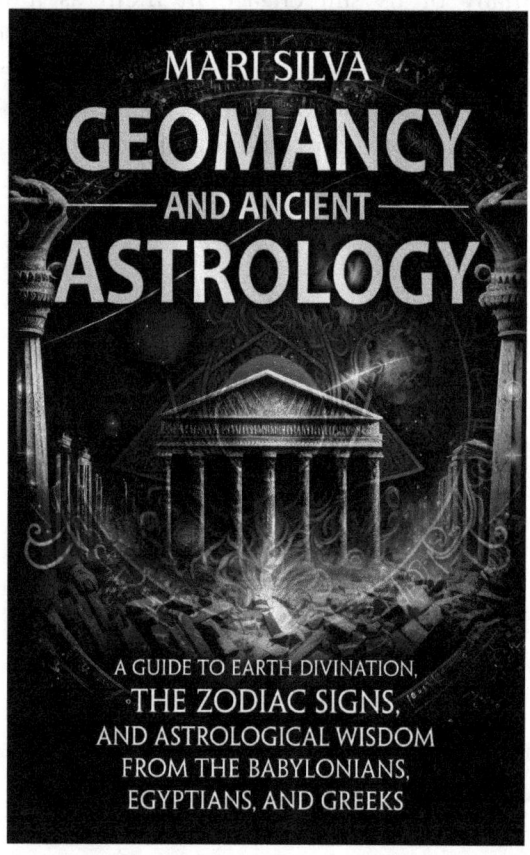

Your Free Gift
(only available for a limited time)

Thanks for getting this book! If you want to learn more about various spirituality topics, then join Mari Silva's community and get a free guided meditation MP3 for awakening your third eye. This guided meditation mp3 is designed to open and strengthen ones third eye so you can experience a higher state of consciousness. Simply visit the link below the image to get started.

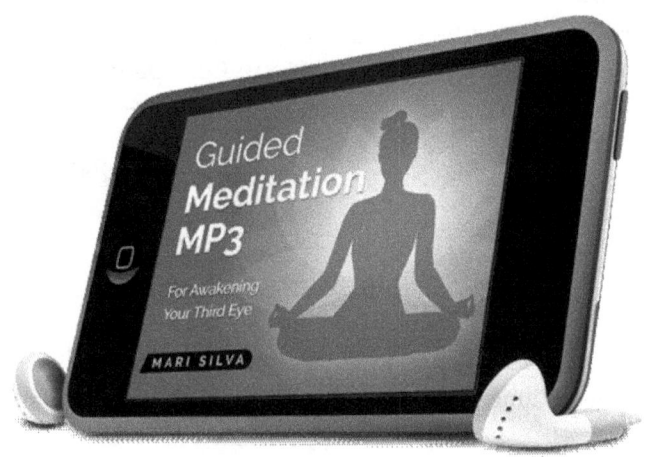

https://spiritualityspot.com/meditation

References

(N.d.). Umich.edu. http://websites.umich.edu/~umfandsf/symbolismproject/symbolism.html/L/ladder.html#:~:text=The%20ladder%20(or%20staircase)%20is,on%20the%20ladder%20of%20virtue.

(N.d.). Usnews.com. https://www.usnews.com/news/best-countries/articles/2017-01-13/13-superstitions-from-around-the-world

(N.d.-a). History.com. https://www.history.com/news/why-do-people-knock-on-wood-for-luck#:~:text=One%20common%20explanation%20traces%20the,a%20stroke%20of%20good%20luck.

(N.d.-b). Usnews.com. https://www.usnews.com/news/best-countries/articles/2017-01-13/13-superstitions-from-around-the-world

10 food superstitions. (n.d.). Walkingpalates.com. https://www.walkingpalates.com/en-UK/10-food-superstitions.php

5 superstitions about funerals and cemeteries. (n.d.). Memorial Planning. https://www.memorialplanning.com/blog/5-superstitions-about-funerals-and-cemeteries

7 crazy food superstitions to digest. (2015, February 5). Farmers' Almanac - Plan Your Day. Grow Your Life; Farmers' Almanac. https://www.farmersalmanac.com/food-superstitions-20419

7 food superstitions you must remember. (n.d.). Christopher-torrevieja.com. https://www.christopher-torrevieja.com/7-food-superstitions-you-must-remember/

8 bizarre food superstitions. (2015, November 14). Tastemade. https://www.tastemade.com/articles/8-bizarre-food-superstitions/

Ablan, D. (2014, April 16). Asbury Park Press. Asbury Park Press. https://www.app.com/story/life/food/2014/04/16/hot-cross-buns-ward-off-evil-spirits/7734891/

ArtDependence. (n.d.). ArtDependence. ArtDependence. https://www.artdependence.com/articles/symbolism-in-art-the-egg/

Arts, G. (n.d.). 18 superstitions from around the world. Google Arts & Culture. https://artsandculture.google.com/story/18-superstitions-from-around-the-world/QQIyTWmzJ9QvLg

Arts, G. (n.d.). Umbrella or parasol? Google Arts & Culture. https://artsandculture.google.com/usergallery/YAISMX_YucmALg

Athira. (2022, September 12). Walking under ladders – meaning of the superstition. Symbol Sage. https://symbolsage.com/walking-under-ladders/

benadmin, & Heath, F. (2017, April 2). Why you MUST wish on a fallen eyelash. Benito. https://benitobrowbar.com/2017/04/03/why-you-must-wish-on-a-fallen-eyelash/

Bhattacharjee, S. (2021, August 26). 7 most common superstitions of seafarers. Marine Insight. https://www.marineinsight.com/life-at-sea/7-most-common-superstitions-of-seafarers/

Brodsky, S., & Schubak, A. (2017, October 11). 55 of the strangest superstitions from around the world. Good Housekeeping. https://www.goodhousekeeping.com/life/g4489/strangest-superstitions/

Celestial Omens. (n.d.). Arizona.edu. http://ircamera.as.arizona.edu/NatSci102/NatSci/images/extomens.htm

Celestial omens. (n.d.). Imss.Fi.It. https://brunelleschi.imss.fi.it/galileopalazzostrozzi/object/CelestialOmens.html

Charbonneau, J. (2022, April 19). Garden folklore: 10 superstitions and traditions. Southern Exposure Seed Exchange | Saving the Past for the Future; Southern Exposure Seed Exchange. https://blog.southernexposure.com/2022/04/garden-folklore-10-superstitions-and-traditions/

Chinese superstitions on colors, numbers, and flowers. (2021, July 19). Han Hai Language Studio. https://www.hanhai-language.com.sg/blog/2021/7/19/chinese-superstitions-on-colours-numbers-and-flowers

Coldiron, R. (2020, September 11). Food superstitions from around the world to add to your Halloween menu. Martha Stewart. https://www.marthastewart.com/7983443/food-superstitions-from-around-world

Cookist. (2020, April 7). Bread turned upside down on the table. Do you know why tradition forbids it? Cookist. https://www.cookist.com/bread-turned-upside-down-on-the-table-do-you-know-why-tradition-forbids-it/

Cowan, D. (2021, August 11). Bad luck for wildlife: 7 Animal Superstitions - Point Defiance Zoo & Aquarium. Point Defiance Zoo & Aquarium. https://www.pdza.org/bad-luck-for-wildlife/

Difference between myth and superstition. (2015, March 28). Compare the Difference Between Similar Terms. https://www.differencebetween.com/difference-between-myth-and-vs-superstition/

Dimitar, D. (2021a, May 25). 10 strange superstitions about babies and parenting around the world (part 1). Babyology-care.com. https://babyology-care.com/blog/post/10-strange-superstitions-about-babies-and-parenting-around-the-world-part-1

Dimitar, D. (2021b, June 1). 10 strange superstitions about babies and parenting around the world (part 2). Babyology-care.com. https://babyology-care.com/blog/post/10-strange-superstitions-about-babies-and-parenting-around-the-world-part-2

Drinkwater, K., & Dagnall, N. (2018, July 2). The science of superstition – and why people believe in the unbelievable. The Conversation. http://theconversation.com/the-science-of-superstition-and-why-people-believe-in-the-unbelievable-97043

Fortune Telling History & Facts. (n.d.). Study.Com. https://study.com/academy/lesson/fortune-telling-history-facts.html

Fuller, M. (2016, August 25). The weirdest superstitions from around the world. AFAR Media. https://www.afar.com/magazine/the-weirdest-superstitions-from-around-the-world

Gallary, C. (2014, November 20). What's a Wishbone, and Why Do We Crack It? Kitchn; Apartment Therapy, LLC. https://www.thekitchn.com/what-is-a-wishbone-and-why-do-we-crack-it-ingredient-intelligence-21302

Google Arts & Culture. (n.d.). 18 Superstitions from Around the World. Google Arts & Culture. https://artsandculture.google.com/story/18-superstitions-from-around-the-world/QQIyTWmzJ9QvLg

Google Arts & Culture. (n.d.). Fortune-telling and superstition. Google Arts & Culture. https://artsandculture.google.com/story/fortune-telling-and-superstition/EgVxiGLYKrypLg

Guide, I. (2018, April 12). Superstitions about travel and good luck. Inspiration Guide; Iberostar. https://www.iberostar.com/en/inspiration-guide/lifestyle/superstitions-how-ensure-good-fortune-travels/

Hale, R. (1518014788000). What's Your Lucky (or not-so-lucky) Number? Linkedin.com. https://www.linkedin.com/pulse/whats-your-lucky-so-number-richard-hale

Harte, J. (2018). Superstitious observations: fortune-telling in English folk culture. Time and Mind, 11(1), 67–88. https://doi.org/10.1080/1751696x.2018.1433357

In honor of Friday the 13th, here are 13 bird superstitions. Have you. (2015, July 9). Audubon California. https://ca.audubon.org/news/13-bird-superstitions

Is it bad luck to open an umbrella indoors? (n.d.). Wonderopolis.org. https://wonderopolis.org/wonder/Is-It-Bad-Luck-to-Open-an-Umbrella-Indoors

Johanne. (2016, June 5). Rice. Good Luck, Symbols. https://goodlucksymbols.com/rice/

Johanne. (2021, August 31). Bread superstitions. Good Luck, Symbols. https://goodlucksymbols.com/bread-superstitions/

Johnson, S., & BA. (2021, March 11). 16 funeral superstitions from all over the world. Joincake.com. https://www.joincake.com/blog/funeral-superstitions/

KADALYS. (n.d.). Wonderful banana tree. KADALYS. https://kadalys.com/en/pages/bananier

Kelly, N. (2013, July 30). Bad-Luck Numbers that Scare Off Customers. Harvard Business Review. https://hbr.org/2013/07/the-bad-luck-numbers-that-scar

Lestz, M. (2017, January 12). Bread and bad luck: A french superstition. Margo Lestz - The Curious Rambler; Margo Lestz. https://curiousrambler.com/bread-and-bad-luck/

Lombardi, E. (2003, August 25). What's the difference between myth, folklore, and legend? ThoughtCo. https://www.thoughtco.com/defining-terms-myth-folklore-legend-735039

Lucky and unlucky numbers around the world. (n.d.). Mama Lisa's World of Children and International Culture. https://www.mamalisa.com/blog/lucky-and-unlucky-numbers/

Mandov, G. (2015, July 1). How to read signs and omens. Inner Outer Peace. https://innerouterpeace.com/how-to-read-signs-and-omens-in-everyday-life/

Martin, G. (n.d.). "Why does bread always fall buttered side down?" - the meaning and origin of this phrase. Phrasefinder. https://www.phrases.org.uk/meanings/butter-side-down.html

Meno, A. (2023, January 26). 15 mystifying superstitions about babies and pregnancy from around the world. Cracked.com. https://www.cracked.com/image-pictofact-9666-15-mystifying-superstitions-about-babies-and-pregnancy-from-around-the-world

MIniac, M. (2015, January 3). Lucky and unlucky numbers from around the world. Sottypong-Review's Site. https://sottyreview.wordpress.com/2015/01/04/lucky-and-unlucky-numbers-from-around-the-world/

Mirror myths & superstitions. (2020, February 5). Two-Way Mirrors. https://www.twowaymirrors.com/mirror-superstitions/

Mulu, R. (2021, June 21). Symbolism and meaning of salt. Symbol Sage. https://symbolsage.com/salt-symbolism-and-meaning/

Numerology: Lucky & unlucky numbers. (2013, March 3). SchoolWorkHelper. https://schoolworkhelper.net/numerology-lucky-unlucky-numbers/

Ottermann, B. (2011, May 22). 13 food superstitions. Health24. https://www.news24.com/health24/diet-and-nutrition/healthy-foods/13-food-superstitions-20120721

Patch, F. (2019, February 19). 40 Filipino Superstitions that You Need to Know during Funerals and Wakes. Flower Patch - Online Flower Delivery Phillippines | ; Flower Patch - Online Flower Delivery Phillippines. https://flowerpatchdelivery.com/blog/40-filipino-superstitions-funerals-and-wakes/

Petrova, E. (2020, February 16). 5 curious bread superstitions you wouldn't expect. Hellenic Grocery. https://hellenicgrocery.co.uk/blogs/blog/5-curious-bread-superstitions-wouldnt-expect

Queaño, P. (2016, April 29). 10 food superstitions in 10 countries. Opodo Travel Blog; Opodo. https://www.opodo.co.uk/blog/food-superstitions/

Raga, S. (2016, May 9). 14 Good Luck Superstitions from Around the World. Mental Floss. https://www.mentalfloss.com/article/79409/14-good-luck-superstitions-around-world

Raymond, C. (n.d.). 13 death and dying superstitions. Funeralhelpcenter.com. https://www.funeralhelpcenter.com/13-death-dying-superstitions/

Reum, Y. (n.d.). Symbolism of mirrors as the first step of individuation and self-awareness. E-jsst.org. https://www.e-jsst.org/upload/jsst-9-1-45.pdf

Rhys, D. (2022a, August 2). 10 superstitions about mirrors. Symbol Sage. https://symbolsage.com/superstitions-about-mirrors/

Rhys, D. (2022b, September 29). Opening an umbrella indoors – how do you reverse its effects? Symbol Sage. https://symbolsage.com/opening-umbrella-indoors-bad-luck/

Saladino, E. (2018, March 6). Why you should never toast with water in your glass. VinePair. https://vinepair.com/articles/bad-luck-toast-water-navy/

Sprankles, J. (2018, June 25). 10 times the celebrity death rule of threes actually happened. SheKnows. https://www.sheknows.com/entertainment/slideshow/9629/celebrity-death-rule-of-threes/9/

Stanek, A. (2022, March 21). 7 horseshoe superstitions still practiced today. Horsey Hooves. https://horseyhooves.com/horseshoe-superstitions/

Symbols, colors, numbers, superstitions, and food. (2019, May 6). Germany Culture Analysis. https://germany789125405.wordpress.com/symbols-colors-numbers-superstitions-and-food/

Tempera, J. (2022, September 14). How to find your lucky numbers in numerology and what each one means, according to experts. Women's Health. https://www.womenshealthmag.com/life/a41124320/lucky-numbers/

Tetrault, S., & BA. (2020, June 5). 17 death superstitions from around the world. Joincake.com. https://www.joincake.com/blog/death-superstitions/

The College of Psychic Studies : Enlighten : Guide to scrying. (n.d.). The College of Psychic Studies. https://www.collegeofpsychicstudies.co.uk/enlighten/guide-to-scrying/

The meaning and symbol of Yogurt in dream. (n.d.). Onlinedreamdictionary.com. https://www.onlinedreamdictionary.com/4389-the-meaning-and-symbol-of-yogurt-in-dream/

Thirteen Animal Superstitions. (n.d.). Advanced Integrated Pest Management. https://www.advancedipm.com/blog/2015/february/thirteen-animal-superstitions/

Timmons, J. (2023, January 5). How To Do A Basic Tarot Reading For Yourself Or A Friend. Mindbodygreen. https://www.mindbodygreen.com/articles/how-to-do-a-basic-tarot-reading

Trujillo, N. (2015, March 19). 9 unbelievable pregnancy superstitions from around the world. Woman's Day. https://www.womansday.com/relationships/family-friends/g1783/pregnancy-superstitions/?slide=1

Turner, B. (2015, July 17). 13 superstitions about numbers. HowStuffWorks. https://people.howstuffworks.com/13-superstitions-about-numbers.htm

Tuttle, R. (2013, February 7). Symbolism of colors and their superstitions. Odd Random Thoughts. https://oddrandomthoughts.com/symbolism-of-colors-and-their-superstitions/

Tuttle, R. (2013, May 19). Superstitions about bread and the baker's dozen. Odd Random Thoughts. https://oddrandomthoughts.com/bread-in-bakery-myths-and-superstitions-about-bread/

Vergara, V. (2021, May 20). 9 superstitions associated with plants and gardens. https://the-line-up.com/; Open Road Media. https://the-line-up.com/plant-and-garden-superstitions

Verma, V. (2020, October 28). 6 popular garden superstitions that you should be aware of. Winni - Celebrate Relations. https://www.winni.in/celebrate-relations/6-popular-garden-superstitions-that-you-should-be-aware-of/

Wagner, S. (n.d.). Try Automatic Writing and Get Messages From Beyond. LiveAbout. https://www.liveabout.com/how-to-practice-automatic-writing-2593046

Webeck, D. (2017, January 18). 13 pregnancy superstitions from across the globe. Stuff. https://www.stuff.co.nz/life-style/parenting/pregnancy/88535413/13-pregnancy-superstitions-from-across-the-globe

Why onion? (n.d.). Onion-Collective. https://www.onioncollective.co.uk/why-onion

Why should you eat garlic empty stomach? (2015, April 18). The Times of India; Times Of India. https://timesofindia.indiatimes.com/life-style/health-fitness/home-remedies/why-you-should-eat-garlic-empty-stomach/articleshow/46957694.cms

Wigington, P. (n.d.). Methods of Divination. Learn Religions. https://www.learnreligions.com/methods-of-divination-2561764

wikiHow. (2011, November 10). How to Get Rid of Bad Luck. WikiHow. https://www.wikihow.com/Get-Rid-of-Bad-Luck

Wolchover, N., & Dutfield, S. (2022, January 28). The meaning of colors: How 8 colors became symbolic. Livescience.com; Live Science. https://www.livescience.com/33523-color-symbolism-meanings.html A folklore survey of county Clare: Animal and plant superstitions. (n.d.). Clarelibrary.Ie. https://www.clarelibrary.ie/eolas/coclare/folklore/folklore_survey/chapter17.htm

Wolfe, S. E. (2021, April 6). Divination Methods for Beginners. Green Witch Living. A beginner's guide to reading tea leaves. Hello Lunch Lady. https://hellolunchlady.com.au/blogs/blog/beginners-guide-reading-tea-leaves

Xing, J. (2022, August 11). 60 common superstitions that people around the world believe. YourTango. https://www.yourtango.com/self/common-superstitions-from-around-world-people-believe

Xing, J. (2022, January 24). Fish symbolism & spiritual meanings of seeing fish. YourTango. https://www.yourtango.com/2020335336/what-spiritual-meaning-fish

www.ingramcontent.com/pod-product-compliance
Lightning Source LLC
Chambersburg PA
CBHW051846160426
43209CB00006B/1180